10 Challenges of a WorldChanger

RON LUCE

OLIVER
NELSON

THOMAS NELSON PUBLISHERS
Nashville • Atlanta • London • Vancouver

Published in Nashville, Tennessee, by Thomas Nelson, Inc., Publishers, and distributed in Canada by Word Communications, Ltd., Richmond, British Columbia.

Unless otherwise noted, the Bible version used in this publication is THE NEW KING JAMES VERSION. Copyright © 1979, 1980, 1982 Thomas Nelson, Inc., Publishers. Scripture quotations marked NIV are taken from the HOLY BIBLE, NEW INTERNATIONAL VERSION®. Copyright © 1973, 1978, 1984 by International Bible Society. Used by permission of Zondervan Publishing House. All rights reserved. Scripture quotations marked CEV are taken from the *Contemporary English Version*. Copyright © by American Bible Society 1990, 1991, 1992, 1994.

Library of Congress Cataloging-in-Publication Data

Luce, Ron.
    10 challenges of a worldchanger / Ron Luce.
        p.   cm.
    Summary: A thirteen-week devotional book to be worked through singly or with a group and which challenges the reader to live what the Bible teaches.
    ISBN 0-7852-7575-4 (pbk.)
    1. Teenagers—Prayer-books and devotions—English.   [1. Christian life.   2. Prayer books and devotions.]   I. Title.
BV4850.L84   1995
242'.63—dc20   95–37405
                                                                  CIP
                                                                   AC

Printed in the United States of America.

6 — 00

TO

A generation of potential heroes
who are teenagers.

This is your moment in history.
Make it count!

CONTENTS

All of the WorldChanger challenges are based on Mark 12:30–31:

> "'Love the Lord your God with all your heart and with all your soul and with all your mind and with all your strength.' . . . 'Love your neighbor as yourself'" (NIV).

ACKNOWLEDGMENTS

There are many people who have influenced my ability to live for God and to write. Hence I will confine my thanks here to those who worked on this project. First of all a big thanks to Joni Jones, who has been typing for me since she was a teen herself. Your sacrifice for this book cannot be measured, and the teens of a generation will reap the benefit! Thank you to Cindy Powell, Charity Virkler, Angie Hinson, and others who worked on this manuscript in various ways.

I owe a great debt of thanks to my precious wife, Katie, and to my family. Thank you for helping me deal with the intensity of getting out of me what God put in me.

ＩNTRODUCTION

This is not a typical book. It's a thirteen-week devotional you can work through by yourself or with a group, but it's *more* than that. It is not supposed to be just one more thing that you read through and then forget what you read. It is designed to get you into action, to push you over the edge to make a big difference in the world.

It is going to be important for you to decide beforehand that you are going to make it all the way through this devotional. The next thirteen weeks could be the turning point that you have been looking for in your life.

I want to encourage you right now to do the following:

1. Make a commitment to have your quiet time every day for the next thirteen weeks.
2. Make a commitment to *do* everything that you are asked to do every day (including filling in all the blanks and memorizing all the Scriptures).
3. Find an accountability friend to go through it with you every day. (Choose someone you feel comfortable with. You need to get in each other's face to keep pressing on every day. The big thing here is to make sure that both of you are doing the stuff every day that you are supposed to do.)

I encourage you to do some pretty wild stuff in this book. Some things will really stretch you out of your comfort zone. Some things will cause you to draw attention to yourself. As a WorldChanger, you have to get people's attention so they know you are a Christian and you are not ashamed of the gospel of Jesus Christ. While I do want you to go forth boldly in every area of your life—home, school, work, sports—I would never encourage you to break any laws or rules set forth by your authorities. You want to avoid offending people so much that you actually drive them away from God rather than drive them into His presence. Keeping this in mind as you read *10 Challenges of a WorldChanger*, get ready to step out of your comfort zone and into the wild, exciting life of a WorldChanger!

I commit to go all the way through this devotional.

I will start on _____ and

plan to finish on _____.

_____
WorldChanger's Signature

_____
Accountability Partner's Signature

_____
Youth Pastor's or Parent's Signature

WEEK 1

A CALL TO ARMS

DAY 1

INTRODUCTION

This book is about becoming a WorldChanger. God is raising up a fresh, fiery brand of young passionate Christians who want to change the world. The purpose of this book is to tell you *how* to become one of them. It is time to wake up. Check out what God is up to and jump into the middle of it!

These WorldChangers are young men and women who take Jesus at His word. They actually believe it is possible to live what He teaches. They have decided to quit just listening to sermons. They have decided to live them. They have decided to go after God with everything in them and to let nothing slow them down.

"What are your plans this summer?"

WorldChangers are determined to make their lives count while they are young. They are tired of hearing prophecies about how God is going to "use young people." They do all they can to *be* the young people God is using now. WorldChangers are not satisfied with just an average, pretty good Christian life where people think they are saints if they stay off drugs. They have something so big in their hearts that they have to *do* something with it or it will eat them alive.

These young firebrands have quit looking to the world for something to do. They are looking to God for their marching orders. WorldChangers find their purpose in Him and in doing what pleases Him. They do everything they can to get the real Jesus into other people's lives because they can't stand the thought of one single person not knowing Him.

Day 2

VALUES

Matthew 6:33

Seek first the kingdom of God and His righteousness, and all these things shall be added to you.

Take four minutes to memorize this verse. Write out what you think it means.

_____

_____

_____

In a very real way, WorldChangers have checked out of this world's system because they value different things. Their hearts don't belong to things; they belong to God. They don't ask what God can do for them; *they ask what they can do for God.* They are not caught up with clothes, clichés, cars, and cool things, but they are turned on to seeking, loving, serving, and knowing Him.

Christianity is not a part-time thing for WorldChangers. They don't go to church because somebody makes them go. They can't wait to get back and dive back into more of God! They have found their identity in Him and in His plan for their lives. They have found the reason they were created, and nothing will stop them.

WorldChangers know that they are here to change this world with the love of Christ.

WorldChangers are here to make this world a different place. They want less sin in the world when they are finished with it. They want fewer broken hearts when they are gone. They want to see more people going to heaven when they are finished pouring their lives out for this world.

They have found something that demands their all, and they don't mind giving it for Him. They have found something worth sinking their teeth into, and they are not about to let go. They have made a discovery so important that it has altered the rest of their lives: You can have all the money, fame, prestige, and toys this world has to offer, but until you have changed the world, you have not accomplished anything.

DAY 3

LOVING GOD WITH ALL YOUR HEART

Becoming a WorldChanger is not complicated or really anything new. It's simply *doing* what Jesus said in Mark 12:30–31:

> "You shall love the LORD your God with all your heart, with all your soul, with all your mind, and with all your strength." This is the first commandment. And the second, like

it, is this: "You shall love your neighbor as yourself." There is no other commandment greater than these.

Take a few minutes to meditate on these verses. Write them out in 1990s teen language.

_____

_____

_____

_____

Amazing, isn't it? You would think that everyone would be doing it already. However, WorldChangers take this command literally. In fact, WorldChangers have had a complete transplant of their hearts. They have a different kind of heart beating in them from the one they had when they were born.

WorldChangers feel a passion to pursue God more than they pursue eating. They have a vibrant, living relationship with Him and refuse to get in a rut with it. They can feel the pulse of God inside their hearts as they yearn to reach the rest of the world. They have surrendered every part of their hearts to God, and they refuse to allow the world back in.

"What in the world are you doing this summer?"

God is the center of their hearts, and they have rearranged all of their priorities. They see the world through different eyes now. They have different goals.

5

DAY 4

LOVING GOD WITH ALL YOUR SOUL AND WITH ALL YOUR MIND

God wants us to love Him with all that we are. Loving Him with our soul is loving Him with our mind, will, and emotions. All of our faculties are wrapped up in loving Him. Let's talk about the mind.

WorldChangers love God with their minds. They have had a transformation in the way they think. They have quit wasting their time occupying their minds with the distractions of the world. In fact, most of the things that the people of the world spend their thoughts on are boring to WorldChangers. They are too smart to let their brains be playgrounds for sin.

WorldChangers are mesmerized by God Himself. They are trying to cram as much God into their brains as is humanly possible without exploding. They think about how to get what they have into other people. WorldChangers think, create strategies, and plan exploits for how they can change the world. They *know* it really is possible to reach the world, so they think through plans to get the job done.

What they have is better than any Indiana Jones adventure flick because what they have is real. They are on an adventure for God, and they have joined Him in coming up with a strategy for an invasion of His love. God needs our hearts and our minds if we are really going to change this world, and WorldChangers know it.

DAY 5

LOVING GOD WITH ALL YOUR STRENGTH

God wants us to express our love to Him by using our energy. He wants you to use your crazy, teenage, wired, frenzied energy to love Him. It's no wonder He wants to use young people—He knows they have a lot of energy to spare.

WorldChangers are constantly looking for another way to use the life within to show the world more of Jesus. They have quit giving themselves to stupid petty things that just drain energy and waste time. Sure, they may still be involved in sports (using some energy), but the real rush is to use their energy for God. They feel that the more intense the assignment, the better.

WorldChangers welcome a physical challenge. They are not mealymouthed, please-don't-make-me-work-or-sweat-because-I-might-melt Christians. They are ready to work their tails off for God—no matter how hard it is. There is no challenge too great for them, no job too hard. There is no mountain too high or river too wide for them to cross. They have counted the cost and are ready to pay it. They will grab that bull by the horns and wrestle it to the ground every time. It does not matter how long or how hard the job is, WorldChangers are up for it. They know it is going to take work if they are really going to change this world.

Day 6

LOVING YOUR NEIGHBOR AS YOURSELF

This is where your challenge lies. Once you have given your all to love Him, He wants you to love the world. It is only in doing so that you will change it. The world cannot help being changed, for it has never seen love like this before.

WorldChangers seek out neighbors. They know that there are plenty of people whose hearts God has prepared and who are just waiting to be told. WorldChangers are ready to seek out the harvest. They realize that it is just as important for others to have the gospel as it is for them to have it. Therefore, they keep going out of their way to get it into others' lives.

WorldChangers will leave their comfort zones and spend free time, even summer breaks, going to where the people are so they can reach them there. They are moved with compassion to find and reach all the "neighbors" in the world and bring the gospel to them.

As you read through this book, you will see a number of quotes encouraging you to think about reaching the world and going on a mission trip. As I have already mentioned, this book is about becoming a WorldChanger, so that means you need to get involved in reaching some part of the world. I know the incredible impact that a mission trip has on young people, and you will never know until you go for it. Let God stir you up as you see the quotes and hear about others' experiences.

DAY 7

A LITTLE BIT MORE

Each day's devotions will fit into one of these four categories: loving God with all your heart, mind, and strength, and loving your neighbor. Each day you will get practical tips for living out the essentials of becoming a WorldChanger. Every day you will be asked to do something during your quiet time as well as throughout the day. Make a commitment now to do it every day. I don't want you just to read about other WorldChangers; I want you to *become* a WorldChanger. It's time to quit talking about changing the world and do something about it. Will you actually do something about your relationship with Jesus?

God is calling the young people of today to do something incredible. He has always used young people when He needed to get a job done in a big way. If you look at David, Jonathan, Daniel, Esther, Shadrach, Joseph, Timothy, Stephen, and John Mark (just to name a few), you can see evidence of God's confidence in young people. Read Joel 2:28,

I will pour out My Spirit on all flesh;
Your sons and your daughters shall prophesy, . . .
Your young men shall see visions,

and see how He is planning the future with youth in mind.

It's time for today's young people to stand up and seize the day. It's *your* turn to make history. It's your turn to shape the world.

This is your chance to make an impact that will be felt for the next one hundred years if Jesus tarries.

This book is about becoming a WorldChanger. It is about loving God. You can have confidence, if you really love God the way Jesus described in Mark 12, that you *will* change the world.

"The path of least resistance is boring. Going on a mission trip is not."

WEEK 2

WORLDCHANGERS IN THE BIBLE

Day 1

DANIEL: KEEP YOUR QUIET TIMES

During the second week of this devotional, we are going to examine several people from the Bible. We'll look at specific things in their lives that helped them to be WorldChangers. I want you to see what you can learn from these biblical examples of World-Changers and look for more as you read through the Bible. As you read about each of these character traits this week, apply the same characteristics to your life.

The first WorldChanger we are going to look at is Daniel. We will refer to the book of Daniel, chapter 6.

Daniel was a young man who lived in a city called Babylon. He loved the Lord with all his heart and kept his quiet times strong every day. In fact, he prayed several times a day. God blessed his life so much that some of the other leaders were jealous because he had so much power. They tried to find something to accuse him of, but "they could find no corruption in him, because he was trustworthy and neither corrupt nor negligent" (Dan. 6:4 NIV).

Daniel was totally, wholeheartedly sold out to the Lord. He was a man of integrity who dealt with honesty and truth. Since they could find no valid means to dishonor him, they made a law that said if you prayed to anyone besides the king for thirty days, you would be thrown into the lions' den. The king, not paying much attention to what he was doing, got suckered into making the law. Since he didn't believe in God anyway, he didn't realize that Daniel prayed that much.

Now here is what I want you to pay close attention to. Daniel found out about the law, and he determined in his heart that he was going to do what was right, no matter what. Verse 10 shows what Daniel is really made of: "Now when Daniel knew that the writing was signed, he went home. And in his upper room, with his windows open toward Jerusalem, he knelt down on his knees three times that day, and prayed and gave thanks before his God, as was his custom since early days."

The first character trait of a WorldChanger is *commitment to God and commitment to quiet times,* no matter what the circumstances. No matter what the situation is, you keep focused on the Lord. You leave the world behind. You say, "People can do whatever they want to do to me. It doesn't matter. I love God with all my heart, and I'm going to do everything that I can to pursue Him with all that I am." Daniel knew that he might even die because he had chosen to keep his quiet times strong, but he didn't care.  Take a moment and list some things here that could distract you from God or get in your way of having your quiet time every day.

1. _____

2. _____

3. _____

Now look at what you have just written. Are any of them as intense as being thrown in a lions' den? If Daniel could be man enough and love God enough to keep his quiet times even in the face of death, can you have enough faith as a potential World-

Changer to stand up to the challenges and not let any of these things keep you from your quiet time? This is your chance to have the same kind of character as Daniel had and to say, "Whatever the world may try to do to me, people may say or do to me, I am going to love my God and come after Him with all my heart in keeping my quiet time every day." Would you make that commitment today and stick with it, no matter what? I challenge you to be like Daniel. Keep your quiet time whatever the cost.

DAY 2

DAVID: WORSHIP

Today we are going to look at David.

Most of the time we think of David as the young guy who killed Goliath. What an incredible warrior he was! That's true. The Bible does say he was a warrior. But I want you to look at something else in his life that made him distinct from the other great warriors.

David was a worshiper. If you are going to change the world, if you are going to do something for God, then you really have to get into worship. When you worship, the presence of God comes. And the presence of God changes the world. He is the One who uses you to do something incredible to make history in this world.

The Bible describes David as somebody who grew up taking care of his father's sheep. He was out in the fields all the time watching the sheep. He used to take his harp with him. As he sat there watching the sheep, he would write songs and sing from his heart telling the Lord how much he loved Him.

David was really into God. He was not singing some cheesy

songs that he had seen on an overhead. He was making them up himself and singing them with all his heart. As a result, the presence of God came on his life to the point that he did incredible things before he even met Goliath.

Look at 1 Samuel 17:34–37:

> **But David said to Saul, "Your servant used to keep his father's sheep, and when a lion or a bear came and took a lamb out of the flock, I went out after it and struck it, and delivered the lamb from its mouth; and when it arose against me, I caught it by its beard, and struck and killed it. Your servant has killed both lion and bear; and this uncircumcised Philistine will be like one of them, seeing he has defied the armies of the living God. . . . The LORD, who delivered me from the paw of the lion and from the paw of the bear, He will deliver me from the hand of this Philistine."**

David is telling King Saul about the things that God had used him to do while he was out just worshiping the Lord. God gave him the strength to overcome a bear and a lion and to kill them both. I want you to realize that it didn't start by David's wanting to kill a bear and a lion. It started when David went after the Lord and worshiped Him with all his heart.

One of the things that marked David throughout his life was that he was a worshiper. We know that he was a major contributor to the most incredible songbook ever to be written in the book of Psalms. David was incredibly creative when he wrote his psalms. He was praising God for all kinds of different things in all kinds of different ways. He was determined to let God hear his heart's cry and his excitement for worshiping. David took particular things in life—the things that other people took for granted like the mountains, the trees, and the blessing he had in his life—and he made whole songs about them.

Take a few minutes and list seven things in your life that God has done for you or that you appreciate that He made in this world.

1. _____
2. _____
3. _____
4. _____
5. _____
6. _____
7. _____

Now I want you to just thank God and worship Him. Really, really tell Him how grateful you are for these things you just listed.

Psalm 119 is the longest chapter in the Bible. David very creatively expresses to the Lord how committed he is to really worship Him. We read things like, "At midnight I will rise to give thanks to You, because of Your righteous judgments" (v. 62). He is worshiping God in the middle of the night. "Your statutes have been my songs in the house of my pilgrimage" (v. 54). David is singing about all the things God told the Israelites to do. Would you be interested in singing a song about the Ten Commandments? David made up songs about loving the Lord with all his heart. He is saying that he loves the stuff God told him to do. "Seven times a day I praise You, because of Your righteous judgments" (v. 164). David is saying, "Man, I'm worshiping You seven times a day for the things that You tell me to do." If you want to be a WorldChanger, then you need to have the heart of a worshiper. You have to be somebody who gives God all the praise and glory and lets Him know that He is your number one passion in life and nothing else even comes close.

Develop the character of David; develop the heart of a worshiper.

Set aside seven times *today* when you can praise God, just like David did, for the things that you just listed above.

DAY 3

LYDIA: KEEP AN OPEN HEART TO THE THINGS OF GOD

The next WorldChanger we are going to look at is a woman named Lydia. You will find her story in Acts 16:11–15:

> Sailing from Troas, we ran a straight course to Samothrace, and the next day came to Neapolis, and from there to Philippi, which is the foremost city of that part of Macedonia, a colony. And we were staying in that city for some days.
>
> And on the Sabbath day we went out of the city to the riverside, where prayer was customarily made; and we sat down and spoke to the women who met there. Now a certain woman named Lydia heard us. She was a seller of purple from the city

of Thyatira, who worshiped God. The Lord opened her heart to heed the things spoken by Paul. And when she and her household were baptized, she begged us, saying, "If you have judged me to be faithful to the Lord, come to my house and stay." So she persuaded us.

As Paul traveled around from place to place preaching, he went to the city of Philippi to take the gospel. He preached for a number of days there. One day a rather wealthy woman named Lydia responded to his message of Christ. The Bible says that the Lord opened up her heart to respond to what Paul was saying. Lydia was a woman with an open heart. She was a woman who was willing to live on the edge. She was a woman who was sensitive to what God was saying, and then she did something about it.

"If you could go on a mission trip free, would you?"

The character trait that we want to note here in Lydia's life is her open heart to the things of God. The challenge for you today is to ask yourself if you *have an open heart to the things of God.* Is your heart open to really hear God's voice every day? Are you open to obey His call to go on a mission trip or change your junior high or high school? Are you willing to live on the edge and do what God has told you to do?

Lydia was. God used her after she gave her life to the Lord to begin a church in her town. It was her openness that helped to start a whole church. As a result, the church in Philippi became a thriving, fiery mob of people living for God. Paul wrote the letter to the Philippian church to follow up on the work he had begun there. That is where we get our book of Philippians in the Bible. Lydia was a woman with a soft heart and the guts to respond.

Will you be like Lydia? Will you have the guts to respond? Will you have a tender heart to God every day? Will you have the boldness to stand up and share with your friends whatever He is speaking to you? Will you stand up and include something of the gospel when you give a report in your class instead of just another oral report? Would you dare have a sensitive, open heart to do what God has called you to do? Will you reach out to somebody in one of your classes who is really hurting and needs to know about Jesus?

Take a few moments and list four or five things that you feel that God has told you in the past to do.

1. _____

2. _____

3. _____

4. _____

5. _____

Now I want you to make a commitment to go back to these things that God has told you to do and go for it. Whether it is witnessing, sharing, or going on a mission trip, commit to go and then do it. Be like Lydia and have an open heart to obey God. Be the first one to respond, even if no one else will. You be the one to change the world by keeping your heart open to what God is telling you.

"Good news! God will pay your way!"

DAY 4

SHADRACH, MESHACH, AND ABED-NEGO: MAKE NO COMPROMISE

Let's look at Shadrach, Meshach, and Abed-Nego.

Those guys were like men of steel. They were in a country called Babylon where everybody worshiped idols. In this case, they were all worshiping a tall idol in the shape of Nebuchadnezzar, the king. Everyone in Babylon had been commanded to worship this idol whenever certain instruments were played. The penalty for disobedience was death by burning. However, Shadrach, Meshach, and Abed-Nego refused to compromise. They refused to give in, even though there was peer pressure all around them. They could have compromised, and no one would have noticed. Yet they refused because they had made a greater commitment to God.

The climax of the story comes in Daniel 3:16–18. Basically, Shadrach, Meshach, and Abed-Nego faced the king and refused to bow to an idol. They told him that they had a living God in their lives. They refused to compromise any of their love for God by bowing down to anything else.

Today in America all kinds of things can easily become idols. There are things that we love just as much as or more than God.

It is a tragedy, but we even bow down to them. You say, "How do we bow down to them?" By giving them our time and by pouring our money into them. We think about them so much, they become idols to us. We end up compromising our true passionate love for the Lord. Even at the risk of their own lives Shadrach, Meshach, and Abed-Nego said, "We will not bow even if it means you kill us. Even if our God does not save us, we will not bow."

The character trait to see in their lives is their *refusal to compromise* by having idols. If you are going to be a WorldChanger, if you are going to do something great for God, you need to have a pure love for God and refuse to have any idols in your life.

Refuse to give your heart to anything like you give your heart to Jesus. Refuse to give your time and your commitment to anything like you give both to Jesus. The thing I want you to see is that the three guys had been taken to a foreign country. They were standing up for God in another country. They were WorldChangers. They were making a difference. They were helping people to see that God was alive. They were showing Him to people who had never had a chance to know Him before.

Take a moment and list four or five things that have been or are idols in your life. Write things that you have concentrated on or spent a lot of time on. Include things that are potential idols in your life.

1. _____

2. _____

3. _____

4. _____

5. _____

Now make a commitment to God to keep your love for Him pure. Promise always to keep these other things a far distant second, third, or fourth place in your life. If they are already idols in your life, then cast them down. Become just like Shadrach, Meshach, and Abed-Nego. Make a commitment that no matter what happens to you or what people say, you will refuse to compromise anything in your life or in your walk with God.

DAY 5

TIMOTHY: HAVE A SERVANT'S HEART

Today we are going to look at the life of Timothy.

Timothy was a young man who grabbed ahold of God and served Him every chance he had. He was a guy who was not afraid to bend over backward to work his guts out for God. Timothy was a young man when Paul first met him. We can see in Acts 16:1–3 that Paul could tell right away that Timothy had a heart to serve. Paul wanted to take Timothy with him on his travels. That began a life of adventure for Timothy. The Bible says that he started traveling with Paul everywhere he went.

When Paul and his companions went to Berea, Paul's life was in danger and he had to leave. Silas and Timothy stayed behind in Berea to keep ministering, but Paul left instructions for them to come as soon as they could (Acts 17:13–15). When Silas and

Timothy came from Macedonia to Corinth to meet up with Paul, they took care of other matters so that Paul could do all the preaching. Timothy and Silas were getting all the rest of the work done (Acts 18:5).

Acts 19:22 tells that Paul sent two of his helpers, one of whom was Timothy, to Macedonia to minister in his place. So we see that Timothy started to represent Paul. When Paul couldn't go, he could send Timothy because Timothy was such a faithful servant. We read in Acts 20 that Paul included Timothy with him on a major outreach. *Timothy had a heart to serve,* and as a result, Paul could trust him and take him wherever he went.

When Paul wrote to the church in Rome, he indicated Timothy was a fellow worker (Rom. 16:21). He was no longer just somebody who followed him around. Timothy had served so well that he had became a fellow worker.

> **"Make this summer count for eternity."**

In his letter to the church at Corinth, Paul described Timothy as his own son (1 Cor. 4:17). Timothy was not actually Paul's son, but Paul loved him as much as a son because Timothy was so faithful in serving him. Paul told the church to accept Timothy because Timothy was carrying on the work of the Lord (1 Cor. 16:10). Basically, Paul was saying that Timothy was doing the same kind of work he was.

Timothy and Paul later began to work together on the letters Paul wrote to churches. Timothy was a very young guy, probably seventeen or eighteen, when he joined up with Paul. He began by just following him around, serving wherever he could. Soon he was taking over administrative duties, and then you begin to see all the different books that he assisted Paul with. When you read 2 Corinthians 1:1, Philippians 1:1, Colossians 1:1, 1 Thessalonians 1:1, 2 Thessalonians 1:1, and Philemon 1, all these books indicate that Paul and Timothy were both involved. So Timothy became a co-sender and possibly contributor with Paul because he was so faithful in working the ministry.

The character trait that I want you to understand from our study of Timothy today is a *servant's heart*. If you're going to be a WorldChanger, if you're going to do an incredible thing to change the world like Timothy did, you're going to have to develop a servant's heart. When you serve with all your heart, God opens doors for you in ministry: "You know what kind of person Timothy is. He has worked with me like a son in spreading the good news" (Phil. 2:22 CEV).

If you're going to be a WorldChanger, you're going to have to be a servant. Begin by learning how to serve your parents. How can you serve your pastor and church? What can you do to serve? By being a servant, you become great in the kingdom of God.

List three or four ways right now that you can begin serving your mom and dad, pastor, and youth pastor in very specific ways in the ministry.

1. _____

2. _____

3. _____

4. _____

Get it into your heart and mind right now. If you're going to change the world and leave your mark on the world like Timothy did, you're going to have to be a servant. Timothy went on to become a pastor and an overseer of a number of different churches. He was an elder who chose deacons. He helped start new churches all over Asia because he had the heart of a servant.

Will you dare be a WorldChanger and have the heart of a servant? Begin today by doing something to prove that you have a servant's heart.

DAY 6

ESTHER: HAVE A HEART OF COMPASSION

We are going to talk about Esther today and examine the element in her life that pushed her over the edge to be a WorldChanger.

I'm sure you have read the story of Esther's becoming the queen in a foreign land. Many Jews were living there. She was a Jewish woman who loved the Lord. Persecution became imminent when Haman decided to implement a law to get the king to agree to exterminate all the Jews.

Esther was faced with a decision: she could either stand up for her people or stand up for herself. She could choose to gamble her life for the sake of other people, or she could protect her life and do nothing to help other people.

So the crucial question for anyone who chooses to be a World-Changer is this: Do you choose to care more for others than you care for yourself?

Will you care for people like Jesus did? Matthew 9:36 says He had compassion on the crowds. Jesus cared more about people than He did about His own life—even to the point of giving His life.

As you read the climax of the story in Esther 4:11–16, you can see that Esther put her life on the line. She sent a message to her uncle Mordecai,

> All the king's servants and the people of the king's provinces know that any man or woman who goes into the inner court to the king, who has not been called, he has but one law: put all to death, except the one to whom the king holds out the golden scepter, that he may live. Yet I myself have not been called to go in to the king these thirty days (v. 11).

And she added,

> Go, gather all the Jews who are present in Shushan, and fast for me; neither eat nor drink for three days, night or day. My maids and I will fast likewise. And so I will go to the king, which is against the law; and if I perish, I perish! (v. 16).

When you have the compassion of God burning in your heart for people, it will push you to do something, even if you have to risk your life.

The character trait of Esther's life that I want to challenge you with today is a *heart of compassion*.

"Someone in another country is waiting to hear the gospel from your lips."

Do you have a real concern for people? Do you have compassion for the people that you go to school or work with? Do you have a compassion for the people around the world who have never heard the gospel? Does your compassion lead to a real heart-gripping concern and commitment to do something? Are you willing to step out of your comfort zone to do something great for God?

You cannot be a WorldChanger without compassion. When I talk about changing the world, I'm not talking about changing plants and trees. I'm talking about changing the *people* of the world. To change people, you have to have compassion. Begin to pray right now that God will pour out His compassion on you and break your heart for the people around you and those around the world.

Think of some things right now that you could do to show the people around you that you have compassion for them and that you have compassion for the people of the world.

You could share your faith with them. You could buy them a burger. You could go on a mission trip or support somebody going on a mission trip. There are many ways to express your compassion. List some of them here.

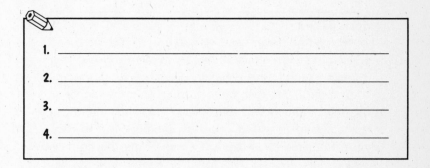

1. _____

2. _____

3. _____

4. _____

Now commit today to implement some of these ideas this week. Show this world that you are not just somebody who talks about loving Jesus. Show people that you love them. Because you love the people in the world, you are going to do something to reach them.

Be like Esther; be a WorldChanger who has compassion.

Day 7

JOSEPH: KEEP YOUR DREAM ALIVE IN YOUR HEART

Today we are going to look at the life of Joseph.

Genesis 37:5–8

Joseph had a dream, and he told it to his brothers; and they hated him even more. So he said to them, "Please hear this dream which I have dreamed: There we were, binding sheaves in the field. Then behold, my sheaf arose and also stood upright; and indeed your sheaves stood all around and bowed down to my sheaf." And his brothers said to him, "Shall you indeed reign over us? Or shall you indeed have dominion over us?" So they hated him even more for his dreams and for his words.

We meet Joseph as a young man seventeen years old. It seems that from the very beginning, he had a dream from the Lord to do something great to change the world.

We know that his brothers despised him because his father loved him more than all the other brothers. They were looking for a reason to hate him. So Joseph has this dream, and he goes and blows his mouth off to his brothers about it. Maybe he should have kept quiet. The point I want you to understand is that he *did have a dream*, and God was speaking to him at a young age. We know the rest of the story: how he was sold to the Egyptians and thrown into slavery. Through it all, he kept the dream burning alive. He was committed to the Lord and to purity his whole life.

It seems that all through his life, Joseph was dealing with dreams. When he was in jail, he began to interpret dreams. Later he was brought before Pharaoh to interpret his dreams. As a result, he was placed as second in command over all of Egypt.

Years after his first dreams, there was a famine in Canaan, and his brothers came to buy grain from him. They bowed down to Joseph, fulfilling the dream you just read about. He had never let the dream die. When he saw his brothers bowing down before him to buy grain, he saw the fulfillment of the dream he had.

> **"For God so loved the world He didn't send a fax; He sent a person. He still sends people today."**

The character trait I want you to get your heart locked into as a result of studying Joseph's life is this: *Joseph had a dream that wouldn't die.*

To do something great for God, you have to have a dream that will not die. It's *not* arrogant to have a desire to do something great for God. Doing something great in the kingdom of God means you're serving other people. You're not getting arrogant and building a name for yourself, but you have a dream to change the world and make it more like God wants it. It's not arrogant to dream a dream for God.

I encourage you to begin to dream big about how God wants to use you in your school. Dream about what you're going to do with your life, your career, and your calling. Dream big. Every summer while you're a teenager go on a mission trip and change the world and minister to people. Dream big. Don't let anything limit you. Don't let money, your past, your family history, or your hometown limit you from doing what God wants you to do. It doesn't matter if anyone from your family has ever gone to a foreign country before. It doesn't matter if others in your family have never done anything great for God. It's not important that no one in your family is a preacher. You need to begin now to dare to dream God's dream for your life and watch what God will do for you.

Take a moment now and begin to dream. If you could do anything for God, if you could be used to do the most incredible things, what would you do? List five things you would like to do for God.

1. _____

2. _____

3. _____

4. _____

5. _____

Now begin to pray over these things; stir up your heart. Ask God to speak to you to confirm these things. Start walking down this path. Don't let the dream God has placed in your heart die, even if it looks foggy right now. As you continue in your quiet times and seek Him with all your heart, it will get clearer and clearer. Make a commitment to go after your dream with all your heart and never let it die.

Be like Joseph; be a WorldChanger. Have a dream to change the world, do everything you can to keep it alive, and watch it come to pass.

I want you to take these seven character traits of a World-Changer that you've learned this week and keep them in mind for the next eleven weeks as you're having your quiet times. Pray over them. Remember Daniel's commitment to have his quiet times. Remember David's heart of a worshiper. Remember Lydia's open heart. Remember Shadrach, Meshach, and Abed-Nego's no-compromise attitude. Remember Timothy's heart of a servant. Remember Esther's compassion and caring for people. Remember Joseph's dream that he would never let die.

Pray over these things every day. Keep them stirred up. Keep them alive as you seek God every day, and develop these other areas of your life so you can be a WorldChanger through and through. It's not just talk to you; it's a lifestyle.

"Missions is . . . 'to go beyond the norm.'"

—Russ

Week 3

Challenge 1:

Commit to Keep Your Relationship with Jesus Alive by Keeping Your Quiet Times

DAY 1

YOU MUST BE BORN AGAIN

John 3:3–8

**In reply Jesus declared, "I tell you the truth, no one can
see the kingdom of God unless he is born again."** *"How can
a man be born when he is old?" Nicodemus asked. "Surely
he cannot enter a second time into his mother's womb to be
born!" Jesus answered, "I tell you the truth, no one can enter
the kingdom of God unless he is born of water and the Spirit.
Flesh gives birth to flesh, but the Spirit gives birth to spirit.
You should not be surprised at my saying, 'You must be born
again.' The wind blows wherever it pleases. You hear its
sound, but you cannot tell where it comes from or where it
is going. So it is with everyone born of the Spirit"* (NIV).

Take three minutes right now to memorize John 3:3 (in bold-
face italics).

In this passage, Jesus is telling Nicodemus there is only one
way into heaven and that is to be born again. Nicodemus, like any
of us might do, asks a simple question: How can somebody enter
his mother's womb and be born all over again? Jesus explains the
answer very clearly and simply.

He says, "No one can enter the kingdom of God unless he is
born of water and the Spirit." You must be born physically—"of
water"—to be eligible to go to heaven, but you also have to be
born spiritually.

If you're alive on the earth, then you have met the first qualification: you were born physically. However, that is not enough. You must be born spiritually as well.

Jesus goes on to say, "Flesh gives birth to flesh, but the Spirit gives birth to spirit." He is talking about being born of the Spirit. The Holy Spirit gives birth to spirit. Verse 8 says, "The wind blows wherever it pleases. You hear its sound, but you cannot tell where it comes from or where it is going." Although you cannot see the wind, you can hear it and see its effects because you see the leaves blowing in the trees.

It's the same way when the Holy Spirit comes into your life. You cannot see the Spirit, but you can see His effect on your life. He changes your life, and you become a brand-new person.

> **"1.3 billion people have never had a chance to hear."**

When you give your life to Jesus, you really come alive on the inside. Your spirit is made brand new, and you're born again. When you make a radical commitment to give your life to Jesus, you believe that He died on the cross for you and rose from the dead. You say, "Now I am going to live for You." A radical transformation happens inside like you were never alive before. Basically, He is saying, "There is only one way to get into the kingdom of heaven. You have to be born into it."

Think of a barking dog. You don't get mad at the dog just because he barks. He was born a barker, and he has to bark because that is the only kind of noise he can make. No matter how much you ask him to stop or how much you spank him, he is going to bark because he was born a dog. Is there any way you could get him never to bark again? You could take out his vocal cords, or he somehow could be born again as another animal, like a cat or something. Now, we all know that is not possible. There is only one way to enter into the cat kingdom: to be born a cat.

It works the same way for people. We are born in sin as sinners. No matter how much we try, we still do wrong things because we are born in sin. The only way to become a person in the kingdom of God is to be born into the kingdom of God. You must be made a brand-new person. That is exactly what happens when you give your life to Jesus. You sell out everything to Him. He makes you a brand-new person. That is what Jesus was trying to explain to Nicodemus.

If you have given your life to Jesus, then it is time to rejoice. You didn't pray some cheeseball prayer. God completely changed you inside out and made you a brand-new person. Take a few minutes right now and thank God for making you a brand-new person. Think about John 3:3 today. Keep repeating it and chewing on it throughout the day.

If you have never prayed to give your life to the Lord, then pray this simple prayer and start your brand-new life today:

Dear Lord Jesus, I commit with all my heart to give You my life. I believe that You died on the cross for me and that You rose from the dead. From now on, I am going to call You my Lord, my Boss. From now on, I live my life for You. You're the center of my life. Forgive me, Lord. Clean out my heart. Clean out my life, and I will live for You every day for the rest of my life. In Jesus' name, amen.

"Missions . . . 'sharpened me as a Christian.'"
—Luke

DAY 2

YOUR RELATIONSHIP WITH JESUS

What is a relationship with Jesus?

John 1:12–13

But as many as received Him, to them He gave the right to become children of God, to those who believe in His name: who were born, not of blood, nor of the will of the flesh, nor of the will of man, but of God.

🕐 Take three minutes right now to memorize John 1:12–13.

The Bible says that if you have given your life to Jesus, if you have been born again, you have become a child of God. You have become a son or daughter of the Most High God, the God who created the whole world, who created the clouds, the trees, the stars, the planets, and the galaxies.

Unlike your physical birth, this did not happen because of some human decision; it happened because spiritually you became a brand-new person. That means you got plugged in to God spiritually. You became connected to Him. You are His offspring, and He calls you a son or a daughter now.

So, you have a relationship with God through His Son, Jesus Christ. You are just like a child to a father. Now He wants to help you grow, to help you be strong, to help you become a mature, responsible human being. Just like a father would provide for his daughter or his son, He will provide food, clothes, and a roof over your head.

God wants to take care of you, nurture you, and help you grow up to be strong. Many people pray and give their lives to the Lord but then continue to do the same things that they used to do, and they wonder why they have problems.

God doesn't want you to pray a little prayer and go on with your life in the same direction. When you pray to give your life to Him, He wants to perform a radical, drastic transformation so that you become just like a little child, a baby in Christ, and He wants to feed you.

He feeds you with His Word. He feeds you by teaching you and filling your life with wisdom from the Bible. He helps you grow and become mature in areas of your life that are not all together, areas in which you have experienced some problems or some bad habits. God is not mad at you. He understands that you were born with a sin nature, but now He has given you a new heart and He wants you to grow up in these areas.

List three areas that you feel you need to grow up in.

1. _____

2. _____

3. _____

The kind of relationship He wants to have with you is one that puts your life back together. Maybe the world has really stomped on you and ripped your life apart in one way or another. God specializes in putting lives and broken pieces back together.

List two or three areas of your life that you feel have been ripped apart and that you need God to help put back together again.

1. _____

2. _____

3. _____

I want you to understand from the very beginning that the Bible says that God loves you like a son or a daughter, and He is out for your best. He wants to take these areas you have listed, and even other areas that you don't know about yet, and help you grow and become mature. Pray about these areas right now:

Father, in Jesus' name, I thank You that You know everything about my life, about my past, my present, and my future. Lord, I commit these areas to You and ask You to help me grow to become a strong man (or woman) of God in these areas. Put my life back together just like a loving father would help his son (or daughter) get strong and mature. I commit them to You, Lord. In Jesus' name, amen.

"You are someone's lifeline to heaven."

DAY 3

LOVE THE LORD YOUR GOD WITH ALL YOUR HEART

Matthew 22:37
> *Jesus said to him, "'You shall love the LORD your God with all your heart, with all your soul, and with all your mind.' This is the first and great commandment."*

Keeping your relationship with Jesus alive is about loving Him with everything in you. It is not about doing things to see how good you can be. It is about loving Him with your whole being. It is not about playing the "church game" or seeing how spiritual you can look. It is about loving God with the very core of who you are.

The relationship He wants with you is one where you love Him with everything you are because you know He loves you with everything He is.

The Bible says that God is love. Anytime you get close to God, you're getting close to love. It's what He is made of. He wants a relationship where you love Him willingly, one in which He loves you and you are able to receive His love.

A lot of people think that having a relationship with God is just following a bunch of rules and regulations and being good so God will love you more. It has nothing to do with that. It has nothing to do with whether you keep the rules or not. He loved you before you ever gave your heart to Him. When you begin to understand His love, you want to love Him back.

God's love is about having a real relationship, a friendship with God, and becoming the person you have always wanted to be and He wants you to be. Because you have fallen in love with the most incredible God of all humankind and realize that He is real, you want to follow Him with all your heart.

> **"Missions is . . . 'becoming the body of Christ to all the world.'"**
>
> —Jeremy

Some people say that they love God, but they do things that are totally against God. They don't really know what they are saying when they talk about love. This is made evident in the way they throw the word *love* around so half-heartedly. They say that they love peanut butter and jelly, pizza, and, oh, yeah, God, too.

Love of God is a different kind of love. It is about loving Him so much that you commit everything to Him. Think about what it would be like for a girl to hear a guy say to her, "I love you, and I really want to marry you." A year later he says, "I love you, and I really, really want to marry you." Five years later he says, "Honey, I love you, and I really, really want to marry you." Ten years later he says, "Honey, I love you so much, and I really, really want to marry you."

After a while, she starts thinking, *Wait a minute! If you do love me, then do something about it. If you really love me, then commit.* That is what loving God is about. It is about loving Him so much that you commit and lock in. When you choose to marry somebody, you're not forced to do it. You want to marry that person because you love the person so much that you want to commit.

That is the same kind of relationship that God wants—that you love Him so much that you commit your life to Him. By your commitment, you agree to live by the principles and the guidelines of the rules that He puts in the Scriptures.

Take a few minutes and write out what you think it means to really love God with all your heart.

_____

_____

_____

Are you living what you just wrote? Are you living the type of love relationship that you read about today? Take this Scripture with you all day long and meditate on it. Ask God how you can love Him today with all your heart, soul, and mind.

CHALLENGE 1: Commit to Keep Your Relationship with Jesus Alive by Keeping Your Quiet Times

DAY 4

WHAT IS A QUIET TIME?

We have been talking this week about keeping your relationship with Jesus alive and about what a relationship with Jesus really is. We know that it is not a bunch of rules, but what is a quiet time?

It is an intimate, face-to-face, heart-to-heart connection with God through His Son, Jesus Christ. A quiet time is the time when you actually build your relationship with Jesus. Specifically, it is a time for you to get up every day and read the Bible and pray and get closer to Him.

A lot of people think, *I prayed a prayer, but I don't feel close to God,* or *I felt really close to God when I was at the Acquire The Fire Convention (or some other retreat or camp), but now I don't feel very close to Him.* You're not going to feel close to anybody if you're not spending time with him.

"Missions is . . . 'giving your time and money to save lives.'"

—Mark

If you were married and didn't spend time with your spouse, the two of you would not grow any closer. Actually, you would grow farther and farther apart.

A quiet time is an expression of your commitment to say, "Lord, I'm going to make sure that I don't accidentally get farther and farther away from You. In fact, I'm going to use this time to get closer and closer to You. I'm going to use it as a time to get fed by You and to get filled up with You and to understand more of You."

Look at John 10:11–16:

> I am the good shepherd. The good shepherd gives His life for the sheep. But a hireling, he who is not the shepherd, one who does not own the sheep, sees the wolf coming and leaves the sheep and flees; and the wolf catches the sheep and scatters them. The hireling flees because he is a hireling and does not care about the sheep. I am the good shepherd; and I know My sheep, and am known by My own. As the Father knows Me, even so I know the Father; and I lay down My life for the sheep.

And other sheep I have which are not of this fold; them also I must bring, and they will hear My voice; and there will be one flock and one shepherd.

In this passage, Jesus describes the kind of relationship He wants. He compares it to the relationship between a shepherd and his sheep.

Now a shepherd and his sheep have a very intimate relationship. Maybe you have this relationship with your pet dog or cat—it knows your voice when you call its name. A shepherd's voice is very distinct to his sheep.

A shepherd walks and hangs out with his sheep. He takes them to different mountains where he knows there is good grass for them, and he really watches over them.

Jesus says He wants the same relationship with you. He wants you to hang out with Him long enough to learn His voice. He doesn't want you to be a stranger He sees only twice a year at Christmas and Easter. He wants to see you often. He wants you hanging out with Him so much that you are listening to the things that He has to say.

A quiet time is a time for you to do just that. You get into the Bible, pray, and just hang out with Him. You pray about the things He puts on your heart, and He speaks back to you. You start your whole day by getting tight with Him.

A WorldChanger is *committed* to having quiet times and to keeping quiet times, no matter what. It doesn't matter how busy you are. It doesn't matter what happens to your schedule.

You are compelled to say, "I *have* to get up. I *have* to pray because I have to get fed. I *have* to get close to my Shepherd, and I don't care what other people do. If I don't get fed from Him today, *I will die."*

I want you to memorize John 10:14 and chew on it all day. Remind yourself that Jesus is the Shepherd and you are His sheep. He knows you, and you know Him.

DAY 5

CHALLENGE 1: Commit to Keep Your Relationship with Jesus Alive by Keeping Your Quiet Times

WHAT TO DO DURING QUIET TIMES

"All right. I get up to have this quiet time thing at 6:30 in the morning. I am up earlier than I am supposed to be. I am a little bit tired. What am I supposed to do during this quiet time anyway?" you say.

Let me tell you. This should be the most revolutionary time of your day. It should be the most exciting part of your day. This is more important than meeting with the president of the United States. This is meeting with the God of the universe, the God who made everything. He wants to meet with you to make your heart more like His, to make your life like His. He wants to do surgery on you and allow you to hear more of His voice and to understand more of who He is, what He is about. It is an appointment with God—something that you don't want to miss.

You can do a lot of things during this time. David described several of them in Psalm 119. You could do one of any number of devotionals, but don't make your whole quiet time just devotionals. They should be just a part of your quiet time. Here are some other things you should do:

* Get into the Word. Begin to read through it. Psalm 119:11 says, "Your word I have hidden in my heart, that I might

not sin against You." You need to hide the Word in your heart. You need to cram it down your throat so that you will not sin.

* Quote the Scripture. Psalm 119:13 says, "With my lips I have declared all the judgments of Your mouth." Talk about the stuff that God is doing. Say it over and over again as if you were meditating on it or memorizing it.

* Meditate on the Word. Psalm 119:15 says, "I will meditate on Your precepts, and contemplate Your ways." Meditating is different from memorizing. Meditating on the Word means you just continue to chew on it and chew on it so you hang on to it all day. (We will talk about that more a little later in the book.)

* Give God thanks. Psalm 119:62 says, "At midnight I will rise to give thanks to You, because of Your righteous judgments." During your quiet times, you need to thank God for His Word and who He is and really worship and praise Him.

* Live the Word. Make a decision to live out a part of the Word that you have read today. Psalm 119:112 says, "I have inclined my heart to perform Your statutes forever, to the very end." In other words, you make a decision that you are going to go for it. You are going to do what you read in the morning. If you don't do anything else, you are at least going to do what you have read this morning.

You can do some very real, practical things during your quiet times. Now I want you to take the rest of your time this morning and read through a portion of Scripture that you choose. Grab ahold of it and be determined. Set your heart on it and commit to do this thing today. Write down the Scripture here. Commit to think about it. Chew on it and live it out today with all your heart.

_____

_____

_____

_____

Let me add that your quiet time does not have to be in the morning. You can do it in the evening or at other times of the day. However, doing it in the morning is a GREAT way to start the day, and it keeps you from getting so busy that you don't get around to it.

DAY 6

CHALLENGE 1: Commit to Keep Your Relationship with Jesus Alive by Keeping Your Quiet Times

JESUS' HABIT OF HAVING A QUIET TIME, PART 1

Mark 1:35
> *Very early the next morning, Jesus got up and went to a place where he could be alone and pray (CEV).*

This is a picture of Jesus' lifestyle of having quiet times. He had an active relationship with His Father; He had to be plugged in to God every single day—it didn't matter how late He had stayed up the night before. It didn't matter what it cost; He got up early and found a way to spend time with His Father.

You see, sometimes we say, "Oh, well, I can still pray with other people around," or "I don't really need to do it every day," but the Bible says that even Jesus got up every day and went away by Himself. He demanded of Himself that He get up to get away from everybody and get tight with His Father.

You may want to live for Jesus and do great things for Him, but the most important thing is what happens in your heart and in your life when no one else is looking. That is what's going to make you the man or woman of God you need to be—full of fire, full of power, and full of conviction to live your life for Him every single day.

WorldChangers know this; they know that they just can't let their mouths flap in the wind and scream "Jesus!" at a conference or convention and then go live *any way* they want. WorldChangers get up and speak to the Lord, *no matter how tired they are*. It doesn't matter what they did the night before. They realize that if they stay up too late, they'll be too tired to focus in the morning. The next night they better go to bed earlier because they have an appointment with God that they *will keep*.

WorldChangers know they can't change the world unless God has changed more of them today. That is what quiet times are about. Get up early just like Jesus did and get tight with God so you can understand what part of the world He wants you to change each day.

If you are not full of God, if your heart is not full of life, then you have nothing to give this world. Sure, you could use some chewed-up Scripture that you used the day before, or you could use some regurgitated sermon you heard someone preach, but God wants you to give *life* to this world today.

To get that life, you need the same habits that Jesus had. Jesus spent a lot of time in prayer. He got up even before the sun rose. In fact, the disciples got up and started looking for Him, wondering, "Where is this guy? Where did He go? We can't find Him. We figured He was so tired from all the work He did yesterday that He would still be asleep."

But He wasn't asleep. He already was up meeting with God. He knew that if He didn't spend time with God, He wouldn't get filled up. Then He wouldn't have anything to give the world that day.

So, establishing a quiet time is establishing a lifestyle and a pattern just like Jesus had. He did it every day. You can do it every day, too. Take some time and get in the Word. Pray and get full of life right now. People need to hear something from you today that you heard from God. However, they are going to get it only if you get connected with God before this day begins.

DAY 7

CHALLENGE 1: Commit to Keep Your Relationship with Jesus Alive by Keeping Your Quiet Times

JESUS' HABIT OF HAVING A QUIET TIME, PART 2

Luke 5:16

> *Jesus would often go to some place where he could be alone and pray (CEV).*

Take four minutes and say this verse one hundred times until you have memorized it.

We are looking here at Jesus' lifestyle of having a quiet time. This is not something He thought about casually, that now and then He might pray a little bit. This is absolute lifestyle. There is no way He could live without it. He demanded of Himself that He get up.

The Bible says that He would often get away to pray. The disciples could not count the number of times. It was not something He did once in a while; it was something that happened so often that they depended on it.

He went to places where He could be alone. Our lives are so busy and so full of activities that we spend very little time alone. We are with a lot of other people or with our video toys, high-tech games, and stuff, and our minds are busy, busy, busy.

I believe that the devil uses all these things—music, movies, and everything else—as distractions to keep us from thinking about God and really getting deep into Him. So, quiet time is when you separate yourself from the world and get plugged in all over again. The Bible says, "Look at Jesus. He was the Son of God, and He got away to pray all the time."

Luke 6:12

Jesus went off to a mountain to pray, and he spent the whole night there (CEV).

Jesus would spend the whole night sometimes just praying to God, getting God to pour Himself out, and getting filled up with God. He shared His heart with God, and then He went out the next day and chose all His disciples.

This whole idea of quiet times is *not an option*. If you want to change the world, you have to be filled with God. You can't go on what you were filled with yesterday. You can't rely on what happened at camp last summer or at church last Sunday. You have to get filled up again today, every day.

God has given you the ability to hear from Him. You have to

let Him pour Himself into you right now this morning. It cannot just be today; it has to be a lifestyle. It has to be so common that even your own family living with you would say the same thing about you that you just read about Jesus: "He always got up and went somewhere to be alone and pray."

If somebody saw everything that you did, he would see your lifestyle habits. He would see that you always sneak away and find God. Some days you have to be desperate to accomplish it.

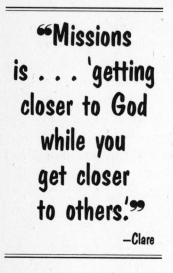

"Missions is . . . 'getting closer to God while you get closer to others.'"

—Clare

When I was going to college, I had roommates. I had to get up very quietly and sneak out of the room because I didn't want to wake anybody up. I didn't want anyone to know that I was praying. Jesus said in Matthew 6:6, "When you pray, go into a room alone and close the door. Pray to your Father in private. He knows what is done in private, and he will reward you" (CEV). I wanted to get the reward that only the Father could give. I just wanted to go off and get more of God in my life. I would stay out late at night just praying and walking around campus and looking at the stars. I wanted so much to hear the voice of God and know His heart and His ways.

It is like a hungering and a yearning from the bottom of your soul. Jesus said, "Blessed are those who hunger and thirst for righteousness, for they shall be filled" (Matt. 5:6). If you feel empty, you need to hunger and thirst for righteousness as you get up and have your quiet times. Cultivate a longing and a yearning for more of God, for purity, for life. Desire to hear His voice so big that He begins to fill you with more and more of Himself.

Too many Christians are empty. They have prayed, but they're empty because they're not hungering and thirsting for righteousness. As you seek God in your quiet times, you need to be hungry. Open up your Bible and say, "God, feed me today." As you look at His Word, He will begin to fill you, and your life will get richer and fuller than you ever imagined possible.

I present to you a challenge this week. If you want to be a WorldChanger, keep your relationship with Jesus alive. Cut off the dead, old, petrified nonrelationship you've had until now. Commit to having a living, exciting time with Jesus every day.

I would like you to sign your name if you will commit to this first challenge as a WorldChanger: keep your relationship with Jesus alive by keeping your quiet times. From this time all the way through your teen years, if you do nothing else, stay in the Word. Keep your walk with God alive by having your quiet times.

I commit to keep my quiet times.

_____   _____

WorldChanger's Signature   Date

WEEK 4

CHALLENGE 2:
Commit Your Mind to God

DAY 1

LOVE GOD WITH ALL YOUR HEART, SOUL, AND MIND

Matthew 22:37

> Jesus said to him, "'You shall love the LORD your God with all your heart, with all your soul, and with all your mind.'"

Jesus said you need to love God with all your soul, which is your mind, your will, and your emotions. What does it mean to love God with all your mind? It means to love Him with what you think, to love Him in what you allow to go through your brain.

A lot of people say they love God with all their hearts, but then they stop there. He doesn't want just your heart; He wants your mind, your will, your emotions, every part of you.

We are going to talk this week about committing your mind to God and loving Him with your mind. You need to say, "God, my mind doesn't belong to me. It doesn't belong to the world anymore. It belongs to You. I want to love You by what I allow my brain to think about. I want to honor You by making sure that the things I think on will give You glory."

God doesn't want to occupy just your heart; He wants to occupy your mind. The world gives you plenty of things to think about, plenty of things that will distract you from thinking about the deep things of God. If He really is the incredible God that He says He is, if He really has made the heavens and the earth, if He really has done all of these mind-blowing things, He ought to be the One who totally lures your mind. He wants to be what you think about more than anything else.

Ask yourself, If people could see all of my thoughts on an overhead projector, would they be able to tell that I really love God? Would that prove that I'm loving God with my mind?

Please take a moment to write down three things that you can think about today to show that you are loving God with all your mind.

1. _____

2. _____

3. _____

DAY 2

RENEW YOUR MIND

Let's talk about loving God with your mind and really committing your mind to God.

When you get saved, you commit your heart to God. You love Him with all your heart, and that's great. Now you need to say,

"Lord, I want You to affect my mind. I don't want You just to affect this invisible heart of mine. I want You to begin to change the way I think." As He changes the way you think, your life will be absolutely revolutionized because it will change the way you live.

Romans 12:1–2

I beseech you therefore, brethren, by the mercies of God, that you present your bodies a living sacrifice, holy, acceptable to God, which is your reasonable service. And do not be conformed to this world, but be transformed by the renewing of your mind, that you may prove what is that good and acceptable and perfect will of God.

The Bible says that you become transformed by the renewing of your mind. I want you to take five minutes and memorize these verses right now.

Some people pray, "God, please change my life. Please change what I do. I'm so sorry." Let me tell you right now that God has already given you the ability to change your life in every area, and He has told you what to do. You say, "Lord, I love You with all my heart." He says, "Good. Now I want you to love Me with all your mind." The way to do that is to put godly things in your mind. He says that your life will be transformed by renewing your mind.

Your mind has been corroded over the years. You live in a world that is full of sin, full of garbage, full of hatred and evil. Everywhere you turn, radio stations, newspapers, magazines, movies, and TV programs offer sin, sin, sin. These things have been crammed down your throat since you were born. But now you have really come alive because you've been born again. You have a new spirit, a new heart. God wants the newness of your heart to affect the way you live by affecting your mind.

Maybe you've prayed a prayer like the one above and then gone out and thought something bad. You may think, *Oh, I guess I didn't really mean it.* Sure, you did. It's just that your mind has been brainwashed with a lot of wrong ideas ever since you were a child. Now you need to renew your mind.

What does it mean to renew your mind? It means to begin thinking God's thoughts instead of the world's thoughts. Think about the truth instead of a lie. Feed your brain the stuff that God thinks instead of wasting time thinking about what you saw on a billboard, a bathroom wall, or a television program. Your life is changed when you begin to think differently, and the way you live is transformed by renewing your mind.

We are talking about making a commitment this week, a commitment to say, "God, I'm going to give You my life. I'm going to give You my mind. I want my mind to be a sanctuary for things that You think, not things that the world thinks. I make a commitment and a decision to put only things in my mind that are going to push me to grow toward You."

DAY 3

THE BATTLE IS IN YOUR MIND

One goal of the Christian life is to live as much like Jesus as you possibly can. You need to get rid of the garbage in your life and to change the way you live so that when people look at you, they get a glimpse of Jesus. You have to put to death the things of the flesh, put to death sinful things, and take on godly and pure habits.

We talked yesterday about your being transformed by the renewing of your mind. You can change the things you *do* by changing the way you *think*. Your battle is not with the things that you do; the battle happens in your mind. If you win the battle in your mind, you win the battle in your actions.

Paul described it in Romans 7:21–23:

> I find then a law, that evil is present with me, the one who wills to do good. For I delight in the law of God according to the inward man. But I see another law in my members, warring against the law of my mind, and bringing me into captivity to the law of sin which is in my members.

Your mind is the go-between. In your heart, you want to do good and holy things. But your body does ungodly things. Your mind is like the referee and hates the things your body does. If you force your mind to think on whatever is true and lovely and worthy of praise (Phil. 4:8), then you will do things that are true and lovely and worthy of praise.

The battleground is your mind. If you are determined to live like Jesus and you are determined to be like Him, then you have to make sure that your thoughts are transformed, that the way you think is more the way God thinks. You do that by cram-

"It's better than free; it's faith that will get you there."

ming the Bible in your heart and your mind. The battle in your mind wages even today. If you want to be transformed today, then you need to begin to think on Scriptures that will help you become strong in that area so that you win the battle.

Take some of the Scriptures you have been memorizing this week and last week. Keep them with you, and think about them all day today. Win the battle in your mind today by keeping God's Word in the forefront of your mind.

DAY 4

HOW TO WIN IN YOUR THOUGHT LIFE

2 Corinthians 10:5

We demolish arguments and every pretension that sets itself up against the knowledge of God, and we take captive every thought to make it obedient to Christ (NIV).

We are talking about how to live a life that is totally committed to loving the Lord your God with all your mind.

We talked yesterday about the fact that the battle is in your mind. Today, we're going to talk about how to win that battle. This verse in 2 Corinthians describes exactly what to do. You have to face the fact right now that if you are going to win the battle in your mind, you are going to have to do something. Today is the day to take action. Take a few minutes right now to memorize 2 Corinthians 10:5.

Let's discuss today's Scripture. It says, "We demolish arguments and every pretension [thought] that sets itself up against the knowledge of God." You demolish anything that pops in your mind that acts like it is more important than God or is an adversary to God.

What does the Bible mean by this? You have to compare anything that comes in your head with the Scriptures. For example, if a sinful thought comes into your mind (*Wow! I want all that money!*), you compare that thought to the Scriptures

("Don't be greedy"). If that thought is setting itself up against the knowledge of God, it needs to be destroyed.

The point is, you don't let every thought that comes into your brain stay in your brain. Some people think, *I don't have a choice. Whatever I think just pops in there.* Well, you don't always have the choice in the first moment that it enters, but you have the choice about whether or not it stays. That's what this Scripture is telling you. It says that you demolish those thoughts; you demand of yourself that those thoughts be destroyed. Don't allow them to stay in your mind.

The second part of this verse says, "We take captive every thought to make it obedient to Christ." Take a moment to write out in your own words what you think this means.

The Scripture is saying that you grab hold of every thought that comes to mind. In other words, you don't just let whatever flies into your brain stay in there. You grab it, and you make it obedient to Christ. If it's not obedient, you demolish it. If it's obedient, you let it stay.

The point is, you have a choice about what goes on in your mind. The more you think sinful thoughts, the more you'll do sinful things. But the more you allow God's Word to infiltrate your mind, the more you'll win the battle over what you do. The more you think holy thoughts, the more you'll do holy things.

It's your choice about whether you choose to let a sinful thought continue to take root in your brain and go into your heart or not. You can choose to demolish it. Today is your chance to demolish ungodly thoughts. But you can't demolish them just by saying, "I don't want them in my brain." You must replace them with something holy.

That's why it's so important to take your Scripture cards (which you'll be making by writing verses on index cards) with you every day so that you can take the Word of God with you wherever you go. Every time you get a sinful thought, take your Scripture card out of your pocket, quote the Scripture in Jesus' name, and put your foot down. In that very moment, you demolish that sinful thought with the Word of God. Today, I want you to take this Scripture (2 Cor. 10:5) with you all day. See how many times you can literally demolish evil thoughts that come into your mind. You, as a WorldChanger, have to take your mind back and let it be a seedbed for the Word of God.

DAY 5

CHALLENGE 2: Commit Your Mind to God

DEALING WITH SPECIFIC BATTLES

I trust you had a victorious day yesterday demolishing and taking captive the thoughts that go against the Word of God. Today, we want to deal in a very practical way with a couple of examples of the battles you are going to have to win.

For example, maybe you have had a problem with anger. You

get mad; you get ticked off; maybe you've cussed at people in the past. Now you're saying that you want to be like Jesus. You know that kind of rage and anger is not like the Lord, so you're going to do something about it.

Remember, the battle starts in your mind. It's not just saying, "I'm not going to get mad." You have to change the way you think. When you change the way you think, you change the way you act.

You can find some Scriptures that pertain to anger. Ephesians 4:26 says, "'In your anger do not sin': Do not let the sun go down while you are still angry" (NIV). You look at Scriptures that say things like, "He

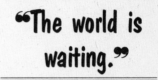

"The world is waiting."

who holds his tongue is wise" (Prov. 10:19 NIV), and you take the Scriptures with you all day long. You begin your quiet time by meditating and chewing on those Scriptures so that when you launch off into your day, you are full of the Word of God.

You already have a stronghold in your mind that says, "I know I am going to live the way God wants me to live." Then every time you are tempted to launch into anger, you pull out the Scripture card and say, "I'm going to be angry, but I will not sin. I will not let my anger control me." That moment is your opportunity to change the way you think, which will change the way you act.

Maybe in some situation in your life someone has really done you wrong. You know you have to forgive her, but you don't really want to. You're mad at her, and you know you should forgive her, but you don't want to, so you keep in the midst of this battle.

You need to change the way you think. Read Matthew 18. Jesus was asked, "How often shall my brother sin against me, and I forgive him?" He said you should forgive "up to seventy times seven."

Jesus then went on to tell the parable of the unmerciful servant. This story describes how the master forgave the servant a huge debt, but that same servant refused to forgive someone who owed him a much smaller debt.

You begin to meditate and chew on that all day long. Then make a decision to forgive, even though you don't feel it. You do it because you know it's right. You continue to chew on the forgiveness Scriptures, and God gives you the power to forgive and gives you the freedom to know what it's like to really forgive.

Today, I want you to use one of these two examples. If you need to forgive someone, or if you've been angry with someone about a certain situation, take these Scriptures and use them to fight the battle in your mind. You will win today, and your actions will change as well.

DAY 6

SET YOUR MIND ON THINGS ABOVE

Colossians 3:1–2

Since, then, you have been raised with Christ, set your hearts on things above, where Christ is seated at the right hand of God. Set your minds on things above, not on earthly things (NIV).

Take five minutes to memorize these verses.

The Bible exhorts you to set your mind and heart on things above. The Bible says that you can choose what you set your mind on. You could set it on the things of the world, you could set it on other people, you could set it on entertainment, or you could set it on having fun, but the Bible says to set your mind on things above. The best way to set your mind on things above is to get your mind into the Word of God.

I want you to notice the word *set*. It is your choice to set your mind on whatever you want to. As a WorldChanger, you have to be an alien and stranger in this world (1 Peter 2:11 NIV). Don't just wear a Christian label. Let God stir up your heart and your mind. Set your mind to aggressively go after the things of God.

Today, you can choose what you will set your mind on—the things of the world or the things above. What are you choosing to set your mind on in your everyday life at school or at work? What are you focusing on? Are you living for what is here on earth and just having a little quiet time in the morning? Or are you setting your mind on the things above throughout the day? Are you saying, "God, I want You to use me. Lord, I want to know You. I want to think Your thoughts. I want to know Your ways"?

Setting your mind on the things above basically is choosing to bombard yourself with the truth, with what is right, with what is holy. For so long, you've lived in this world, and you've been brainwashed with lies. Now is the time for you to immerse yourself in the truth. It's time to cram the truth down your throat.

It reminds me of when I had just been turned on to the Lord. My father and I would go out to work. I would turn the radio station to listen to preachers, and he would turn it to listen to some music. I'd turn it back to preachers. Finally, he'd say, "Son, you just need balance! You need balance in your life." I thought for a while about what he said. I didn't say this to him, but I thought, *You know, Dad, you're right. I do need balance. And I've had so much garbage crammed down my throat from the devil and the world that I'm going to need the Word of God in my mind and in my heart twenty-four hours a day for the* next twenty years just to get balanced. I need to get my mind set on things above.

Use Colossians 3:1–2 as a reminder all day to get your mind set on things above. Anytime you have free time, anytime your mind starts to wander, take this Scripture out and start to meditate on it and memorize it.

Choose today to set your mind on things above. I know it sounds different and it sounds wild, but you're not an average Christian—you're a WorldChanger.

DAY 7

CHALLENGE 2: Commit Your Mind to God

YOU HAVE THE MIND OF CHRIST

---

1 Corinthians 2:9–10
However, as it is written:

> "No eye has seen,
>   no ear has heard,
> no mind has conceived
>   what God has prepared for those who love him"—

but God has revealed it to us by his Spirit. The Spirit searches all things, even the deep things of God (NIV).

1 Corinthians 2:16
  For "who has known the mind of the LORD that he may instruct Him?" But we have the mind of Christ.

The Bible is describing a mind that is totally committed to God. This is what you can expect. First of all, it says, "No eye has seen, no ear has heard," no one has even thought of what God has prepared for us.

The average Joe walking down the street could never imagine how incredible the stuff is that God has prepared for us. However, verse 10 says, "God has revealed it to us by his Spirit." He has revealed the incredible, wild things that He wants to do in us, through us, and to us by His Spirit. But only people who have His Spirit are going to get this revelation.

Then He says that we have the mind of Christ. As you begin to put more and more of the Bible in your mind, you think more like God because the things He said are rolling around in your mind. As you train your mind to think the way God does, you begin to think like God thinks, and you get the mind of Christ. God will speak some very incredible things to you regarding what He wants to do in your life and through your life. He'll explain to you how He wants to use you to change the world and set people free, to change whole villages, communities, states, and countries.

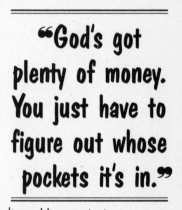

"God's got plenty of money. You just have to figure out whose pockets it's in."

God will speak to you and tell you how He wants to use you because your mind has been trained; it is like the mind of Christ.

Some Christians wonder why God never speaks to them. The problem is that they haven't trained their minds to think like God thinks. Maybe God is speaking to them, but they don't understand it because they still think like the world thinks. Sure, they committed their hearts to God, but they never committed their minds. As a result, the things God wants to do in their lives are still a mystery to them. They continue to think, *Maybe God will lead me someday.* It becomes a vague journey for them.

I want to encourage you to make a commitment—not just for this week, and not just for the duration of this devotional book, but for at least the rest of your teen years—to commit your mind to God, to choose to focus on things above. As you do this, you will begin to get the mind of Christ and hear the voice of God. It's a radical difference from the way the average person thinks.

If you're going to change the world, you have to begin by changing yourself. You'll be amazed as you watch yourself become more and more like God. As you begin to change the world, you will change it more into the way God wants it because you can think the way God thinks. He has changed your mind and your heart. As a result, He has changed your actions, and you will change the world.

I hereby commit my mind to the things of God. I commit to regularly memorize and meditate on Scripture. I will cram the Word in my brain, take captive any thoughts that would go against the will of God, and set my mind on things above, so that I can have the mind of Christ and change the world like He wants me to.

_____   _____
WorldChanger's Signature   Date

Week 5

Challenge 3:
Commit to Systematic Bible Study

DAY 1

JESUS IS THE WORD

John 1:1–2

In the beginning was the Word, and the Word was with God, and the Word was God. He was in the beginning with God.

John 1:14

The Word became flesh and dwelt among us, and we beheld His glory, the glory as of the only begotten of the Father, full of grace and truth.

The Bible says that the Word was in the very beginning, that the Word was with God, and that the Word actually was God. It is important for you to study the Bible, which is the Word of God, on a regular basis. I want you to really understand what the Word of God is all about.

As a WorldChanger, you can't haphazardly "sort of" get into the Bible; you've got to get into it with all your heart and soul. A word is not merely something that somebody says. The essence of a word is an expression of a thought.

Whenever God speaks something, He expresses what He already thought about beforehand. When you read that the Word was with God and the Word was God, you see that what God was thinking He began to speak about. Whenever God spoke, wild things happened.

He said, "Let there be light," and the sun exploded in mid-air.

He said, "Let there be stars . . . earth . . . plants . . . ," and they all came to be. God thought it, He said it, and then an amazing thing happened: it just exploded. That is how powerful God's words are.

The Bible goes on to say that the Word became flesh and dwelt among us. In other words, what God was thinking became flesh. We know this is His Son, Jesus Christ. Colossians 1:15 says that Jesus is "the image of the invisible God." If you want to know what God is thinking, look at Jesus. *He is the expressed image of the invisible God.* He is the Word made flesh.

"Missions is . . . 'giving the world the greatest gift of all.'"

—Joey

Why is it so important for you to know God's Word? Simply this: as you read and study the Word, you discover what God is thinking. You read His Word, which is the expression of His thought. So if you want to get inside God's mind, inside God's heart, begin to read God's Word, and you'll find out what He is thinking about.

If you read His Word, you'll begin to understand what is going on in His mind. You'll begin to know exactly what He is thinking about. Ninety percent of all the questions you would ever want to ask God are answered right in His Word. You've just got to realize how valuable the Bible is.

This week we are going to be talking about getting the Word of God in your life on a regular basis. This is directly linked to committing your mind to God, just as we talked about last week. Now, instead of your mind being committed to the world, it's committed to the Word. To be committed to the Word, you've got to really study it. As you do, it will feed your spirit and help you grow into a strong person of God.

As a WorldChanger, you've got to be serious about really getting to know God. The more you get to know His Word, the more you get to know His thoughts, and the more you get to know Him and what He's really like.

Take some time today to really think about God's Word. Carry around cards of the verses you've memorized so far, and realize that these are God's thoughts you're memorizing. What He was thinking, what was going through His mind and His heart, is what you are memorizing as you take these Scriptures to heart.

CHALLENGE 3: Commit to Systematic Bible Study

DAY 2

THE VALUE OF READING THE WORD

---

2 Timothy 3:16–17

All Scripture is God-breathed and is useful for teaching, rebuking, correcting and training in righteousness, so that the man of God may be thoroughly equipped for every good work (NIV).

Take three minutes and memorize 2 Timothy 3:16–17 right now.

We're going to talk about the value of reading the Word and why it's so important. I've already mentioned that it helps to renew your mind because you're reading and memorizing what God thinks. This passage in 2 Timothy talks about the fact that all Scripture is inspired by God—it came out of His heart. It's valuable for several specific things in your life.

First of all, it's useful for teaching. The more you read the Word, the more God will begin to teach your heart. Teach you what? God's Word will teach you how to live in this world, how to be successful, how to prosper, how to have vision, how to have a dream, how to fulfill your dreams, how to manage finances, how to conduct friendships or relationships, how to deal with marriage, and how to be the WorldChanger God wants you to be. The Word teaches you how to live.

The world teaches you how to live in a wrong way. Anything good the world happens to teach happens because it lines up with the Word of God. Why try to sift through all the junk in the world? Just go straight to the Word. You will learn principles that will teach you how to live and how to pull your life together.

Name a couple of areas of your life that you would like God to really teach you about.

1. _____

2. _____

God's Word is also valuable for rebuking and correcting. There may be things in your life that need to be rebuked and corrected. As you read the Word of God, it will instruct you and correct you; it will show you the right way to do things.

You'll read a Scripture—a story or parable Jesus is telling, or an example in the Old Testament—and all of a sudden you'll go, "Wow, that's happening in my life." That's exactly what Paul means in 2 Corinthians 3:16 when he says, "When one turns to the Lord, the veil is taken away."

Maybe you'll feel rebuked by the Lord: "Hey, buddy, you need to get this part of your life together." When you feel that, you should say, "Okay, Lord, I'm listening." Then repent and commit to memorize that Scripture and meditate on it until your life lines up with the Word.

Take a moment here and write out a couple of areas that you feel need to be corrected in your life. They can be from the Scriptures you've already memorized or stuff you know from the Bible, areas you feel God wants to rebuke or correct in your life.

1. _____

2. _____

The Scripture also says that the Word will train you in righteousness. This world trains you in unrighteousness. It teaches you in the way everyone lives and the examples of an unholy, ungodly, unrighteous life. The Word of God teaches you with positive examples, encouragement, rebukes, and exhortation how to live righteously in an unrighteous world.

It teaches you so that you can be equipped for every good work. God is expecting you, as a WorldChanger, to do a lot of good works, and your good works will change this world. As you cram the Word of God down your throat, He equips you and gets you ready to do all the incredible things He wants you to do to change the world.

Spend some time in the Word today seeking some of the things you want God to teach you about. Write 2 Timothy 3:16–17 on an index card, and carry it with you all day long as you deal with areas you feel God wants to correct.

DAY 3

WHAT TO LOOK FOR WHEN YOU READ THE WORD

When you read the Bible, make sure that it doesn't become just another book. It must not become the obligatory "I've got to read a couple of chapters today because of my commitment" thing. You want to really look for how God wants to speak to you through specific things in His Word. Let me give you a couple of things to look for every day as you read.

First of all, as you are getting ready to read any book in the Bible, read the introduction to it. Most Bibles you buy today will have a little bit of an introduction to tell you about the author, why he wrote the book, when it was written, and so forth. That can help you understand more of what is going on in the book you are about to read.

As you begin reading, think about the people the book was written to. Ultimately it was written to you because, by the Holy Spirit, God speaks to all of us.

However, take time to think about the original audience. Did Moses write that book? Who were the people he wrote it to? Did Paul write it? When Paul wrote the book of Corinthians, who were the people he wrote to? These questions (and their answers) can help you understand more specifically why the author said some of the things he said.

For example, First and Second Corinthians were written to the church in Corinth, which was living in sin. He was telling them specific things about how to fight the sin there.

The next question to ask is, Why did the author write it? Did Paul write his letters because he was so bored in jail, or was he writing to get a specific point across? If you understand the author's purpose, you'll understand more of what you read.

Turn to the book of Luke. In chapter 1, he states that he wrote that book to give a very accurate picture of who Jesus was. He was not writing to everybody; he was writing to his friend. He wrote a letter of Jesus' life to a friend, and we ended up getting that letter and publishing the book of Luke in the Bible.

The final question is, What did it mean to the original audience? Sometimes we find a Scripture and take it out of context, and we don't really know what the writer was trying to say. We make it say something that the author never meant it to say. Try to put yourself in the mind-set of the people to whom the book was written. Think of what was going through their minds the first time they heard it. As you think about what it meant to them, you may be able to understand more of what it means to you.

Why don't you try this today? Go back and read the introduction to whatever passage of the Bible you are reading today. When you read the chapter you are on, think about who wrote it, the people he wrote it to, why he wrote it, and what it meant to the original audience. You'll be amazed at the insights you'll get.

"Are you consumed by the mall or consumed by the call?"

DAY 4

HOW TO GET THE MOST OUT OF THE WORD EVERY DAY

We're talking about being a WorldChanger. A WorldChanger has to be someone who is absolutely transformed and changed on the inside by the Word of God. If you're going to change the world, you have to be changed first. Otherwise, you have nothing to offer the world.

Today, we're going to talk about some very specific things that will help you get a lot out of the Scripture as you read it.

Psalm 119:15–16

I will meditate on Your precepts,
And contemplate Your ways.
I will delight myself in Your statutes;
I will not forget Your word.

We've already talked about the Bible as God's thoughts. When you read the Bible, you're reading God's thoughts. Let me discuss it from a little different perspective.

We are talking about having a relationship with God. The problem is, how do you have a relationship with someone you can't see? How do you get closer to somebody if you can't see how close you are now? How do you know if you really know somebody well? After all, isn't that what a relationship is about?

Think about one of your friends. How can you tell whether you really know a friend well? Is it because you are physically close to him? You could sit next to him every day in geometry and not know him at all. But this is the way a lot of people think.

How do you get to know God? Compare this to how well you know one of your friends. If you know someone really well and somebody else accuses her of something you know is not true, you can say, "No way, I know that's not true." You know it's a lie because you know that person—you know she would never do that.

So what does it really mean to know a person? It means you know her character, what she's like on the inside, what she's made of. You know whether she would ever do the things she's been accused of.

That is exactly what I'm talking about when I say you need to get to know God. He's invisible, so you can't see Him, but that doesn't mean you can't get to know Him. Getting to know God means getting to know His character, His personality.

David talks about this in the psalms. He says, "I will meditate on Your precepts, and contemplate Your ways." He goes on all the way through chapter 119. He says, "I think about Your ways, Your principles, and Your statutes." In other words, when God does something, He always does it the same way. That is what a principle is. As you learn about God's principles, you learn more about Him. You learn to say, "Lord, I love Your precepts. The more I get to know Your laws, the more I get to know what You are really like."

Reading the Bible is not just going through it and reading a verse here, a story there. It's actually going on a *quest for God*. Every single day you wake up saying, "God, I love Your principles. I love Your precepts. I want Your ways."

In every chapter of the Bible you read, you should be asking this huge question: What can I learn about God's character? Ask yourself, What can I learn about the way He does things? How can the way He treated somebody or the way He did something be a guiding principle in my life? What does it mean to me that He delivered someone from his enemies?

That is what you want to take with you every single day. As you get up and dive into the Word, you say, "God, I'm on a quest for You. I'm getting to know more of You. I'm abandoning the world. I'm grabbing hold of You, and I'm finding more of You today."

This morning as you dive into the Word, read a chapter or two, and ask yourself, What can I learn about God's character, His nature, and His principles? Grab on to just one of those things today. If you can grab hold of just one principle of what God is really like each day, you will have the most incredible life because you will be getting to know Him better and better every day.

DAY 5

CHALLENGE 3: Commit to Systematic Bible Study

MEDITATE ON THE WORD OF GOD

As we learned yesterday from Psalm 119:15–16, David loved the Word of God. He meditated and chewed on it. In verse 24, he said, "Your testimonies also are my delight and my counselors." He delighted in chewing on the Word. He said in verse 48,

> My hands also I will lift up to Your commandments,
> Which I love,
> And I will meditate on Your statutes.

He said it again in verse 97, "Oh, how I love Your law! It is my meditation all the day." David was saying, "I just meditate and chew on the Word."

Meditation is not the same as memorization. When you memorize something, you just quote it. When you meditate on something, you chew on it and you chew on it, just like a cow chews its cud. Cattle have a stomach with four compartments. When they eat, they chew their food only enough to swallow it. It's broken down some and later is coughed up. Then it's chewed on some more and swallowed again.

That is exactly what you're doing when you meditate. You're chewing on God's Word and chewing on it; it's stirring you up and you keep chewing on it and chewing on it. When you've chewed on it long enough, you begin to be able to digest it, just like a cow does. After doing this for a while, it becomes alive to you. It's not just a boring little Scripture; it's real because you've chewed on it enough for it to sink into your mind. So the question for each day is, What Scripture are you chewing on?

The Bible describes this concept in a different way in Ephesians 5:26. It talks about washing your mind with the water of the Word. As you meditate, your mind begins to get washed and washed and washed with truth. All the brainwashing the world has done to you begins to get washed away, and your mind gets cleaned up. It's a choice that you make; you don't accidentally get washed with the Word. You've got to choose, just like David did, to meditate and meditate and chew and chew on one Scripture and let it really sink down into your heart and mind.

Meditating on God's Word is a great habit to get into because then it isn't just another story you read that morning. It's life for you. It's real food for you that triggers your heart to believe that it's true. The scales fall from your eyes, and God's Word sets you free. It comes alive to you.

Choose a Scripture today—maybe one of the Scriptures that you have already memorized during this study. I want you to chew on it like you have never chewed on anything before in your life. Every spare moment you have, I want you to chew and chew and chew, repeat it again and again to yourself, over and over. Then watch out and see what God does in your heart today!

DAY 6

CHALLENGE 3: Commit to Systematic Bible Study

APPLY THE WORD OF GOD TO YOUR LIFE

I hope you had a great day yesterday as you chewed on the Word. We're going to talk about how to apply the Scripture specifically to your life.

Hebrews 4:12

For the word of God is living and active. Sharper than any double-edged sword, it penetrates even to dividing soul and spirit, joints and marrow; it judges the thoughts and attitudes of the heart (NIV).

Take five minutes and memorize this Scripture. Work on it until you can say it five times in a row without looking.

The Bible describes the kinds of things the Word of God can do in your life. It says the Word of God is not just some boring book that somebody else wrote. It's living, and it's active. The thing the world doesn't understand about the Bible is that *it's alive and active.*

If you meditated, really meditated, on the Word yesterday like we talked about, you probably discovered how alive and active the Word is. It's so alive that it can pierce your heart, deal with things in your life, and change your life like nothing else can. As you learn to apply specific Scriptures to your life in areas where you're struggling, you're confused, or you're overcoming sin, you begin to realize how active His Word is, how alive it can really be.

Every day as you read a portion of the Scriptures and begin to discover who God is and what He's like, ask yourself several questions: What is this saying to me today? How can I apply what God is saying here to my life today? What is He telling the original audience, and how does it apply to my life? If I were there living in the time this Scripture was written, what would I need to take into my heart and ask God to change in me?

The Word of God is also living and active in areas of your life that you know you need to change but you don't know how to change them. Remember our discussion earlier, about getting transformed by the renewing of your mind? You cram the Bible in your mind about that particular issue, and it begins to change your mind and then your actions.

I've talked to many people with specific problems in their lives. They've gone to counselors and tried to work through problems with their parents or emotional problems. They have spent a lot of money but haven't gotten any answers. They're so discouraged because they can't get over their problems.

Then all of a sudden they get into the Bible, and because the Bible is living and active, it changes their lives. It's not just another philosophy book. It's the Word of God. You get enough of it in your life and it changes you; it literally changes you.

Believe me—I've seen them, and I've talked with them. They get set free. After spending thousands of dollars on counselors, they are set free by getting into the Word and letting God change their lives by His free gift. Of course, there are many who are helped by counseling, but it is important to remember that it's the truth, not psychology, that sets you free.

I want you to take a moment and list some areas of your life that you know need to change. God probably has spoken to you in the past about them. Maybe they're sinful thoughts, sinful desires, or sinful actions. Take a moment and write them here. Just concentrate on the problem areas first—we will fill in the Scriptures later.

1. _____

_____

Scriptures: _____

2. _____

_____

Scriptures: _____

3. _____

_____

Scriptures: _____

4. _____

_____

Scriptures: _____

Now I want you to get your Bible and find some Scriptures that apply to each of these areas. If you have a problem with sin in a specific area, go to a concordance or ask your pastor or somebody else who is trustworthy for a Scripture that will tell you how to deal with that area. For example, you could begin with the forgiveness Scriptures that we talked about last week.

Choose one of the areas you listed above, and write out the Scriptures you've found to go with it. Now meditate on them, chew on them, and let them become alive to you so you can apply that area of the Word to your life today. Watch the transformation begin!

CHALLENGE 3: Commit to Systematic Bible Study

DAY 7

KNOW THE WORD

As a WorldChanger, you've got to realize you have to be a living, breathing Word machine. Devour the Word of God. Let it transform your brain. Cram it down your throat, and let it begin to stir up your insides.

I don't care whether you are thirteen, fourteen, seventeen, or eighteen years old. Age doesn't matter. It's time right now to change the way you think, to think more like God. You need to live more like Him as His Word becomes alive inside you.

Another essential element to stand strong as a WorldChanger is to read the Bible all the way through on a regular basis. Don't just open the Bible and say, "This must be where God wants me to read today." You need to read through the whole Bible again and again and again.

You don't have to go through the whole Bible this week, but you do need to begin now. Decide that you're going to read one book a week or a month or something—just set a goal now.

Do something to really get the Word inside you. Start at the beginning and go all the way through. It might take you a year or two, but you've got to make the decision right now not to be an airhead Christian who knows only a little about the Bible. Dive into it and really know it. Don't think you know it because you heard your pastor preach it to you. You need to know it for yourself.

You need to know the order of events. Did King David come before King Solomon or after King Jehoshaphat? Did Moses come before or after David? Learn the history and the order of how God did things, and you'll learn a lot about the character and nature of God.

There are Bible reading plans available that you can use if you want to read the entire Bible in a year. I believe you can do it. I've seen thousands of young people make a commitment to read the Bible in a year and follow through with it.

Even if you don't make this full commitment, you should at least commit to going halfway through the Bible or several books a month so that you can aggressively pursue how God thinks and who He is.

If you're going to change the world, you've got to be aggressively into the Word of God.

I commit to seek out the character of God, to meditate on it and let it become alive to me, and to systematically read through the Bible so I get all the way through the Bible at least one time during my teen years (I hope this year).

_____   _____
WorldChanger's Signature   Date

Week 6

Challenge 4:
Commit to an Accountability Friendship

DAY 1

WHAT IS AN ACCOUNTABILITY PARTNER?

What is an accountability partner? The definition of *accountability* is "obliged to account for one's acts, being responsible, capable of being accounted for" *(Webster's New Collegiate Dictionary, Tenth Edition)*. Having an accountability partner is letting someone else be in a position where you can give an account of your life before him or her.

Proverbs 17:17
*A friend loves at all times,
And a brother is born for adversity.*

An accountability partner or friend is someone you trust to love you at all times—in the good times as well as the bad times. He would love you when you are on rocky ground and when you are sailing victoriously.

One of the problems a person encounters when she commits her life to Christ is that many times she continues to surround herself with people who do not love the Lord. She feels like she can't be herself around other people and really let them know everything going on in her life. If she does something to really blow it in her walk with God, she keeps it to herself and begins to develop a list of secret sins.

An accountability friend will love you whether you do right or wrong. He loves you too much to let you do bad things and do nothing about it. Instead, he will kick you in the backside and help you get your act back together.

As a WorldChanger, you cannot afford to be a Lone Ranger Christian. Christianity is not about coming forward to the altar, crying and praying, hoping you can change your life by yourself. It's about getting locked in with other people who have the same fire and passion to change the world.

> **"Have you prayed for the unreached people of the world lately?"**

Christianity is about locking hearts with people and saying, "We love each other too much to let each other backslide. We love each other too much to let each other get into sin and not say something about it." It's about getting in each other's face and helping each other go for God.

If you try to ride off like a Lone Ranger Christian, you make yourself a really easy target for the devil to pick off. You must lock arms and lock hearts with several other people who are committed and accountable to each other and say, "If you see anything in my life that doesn't look like Jesus, I want you to tell me about it. I want so much to look like Jesus, I don't want anything to accidentally get in my life that I don't deal with." That is what accountability friendship is all about.

A real friend will love you at all times, even though she might see something that is not going very well in your life. She'll love you enough to tell you about what's going on. It's not about judging each other; it's about being committed in good times and bad.

Meditate on Proverbs 17:17 today. Begin to pray and ask God for an accountability friend or two who can really push you to be more like Jesus.

DAY 2

THE VALUE OF AN ACCOUNTABILITY PARTNER

Galatians 2:11–14

When Peter came to Antioch, I told him face-to-face that he was wrong. He used to eat with Gentile followers of the Lord, until James sent some Jewish followers. Peter was afraid of the Jews and soon stopped eating with Gentiles. He and the others hid their true feelings so well that even Barnabas was fooled. But when I saw that they were not really obeying the truth that is in the good news, I corrected Peter in front of everyone and said: "Peter, you are a Jew, but you live like a Gentile. So how can you force Gentiles to live like Jews?" (CEV).

An accountability partner keeps you from getting off track and doing wrong things. Some things might seem right in your eyes, but according to Scripture, they are not right (Prov. 21:2). It's not about judging each other and getting mad at each other. It's about helping each other go toward the Lord, and going hand in hand.

Here in Galatians you can see a very specific example of this kind of accountability. Basically, Paul got in Peter's face and said, "You're being a hypocrite. You're saying that you're not better than these guys, but then you eat only with the Jews and not everyone else." Paul faced him right in front of everybody.

That doesn't mean that if you are an accountability partner, you need to face your friend or embarrass him in front of everyone, but you need to be honest enough to speak the truth to him. As an accountability friend, you can't force someone to change, but you can definitely draw him to account.

Paul said, "Peter, this is not right. And if you think it is, I need you to give me an account. Explain to me why you are doing this if you think it is so right." If your friend can't give an account for her actions or attitude, she should be prepared to admit that she is wrong and commit to change.

Having an accountability partner is very scriptural and godly. In fact, it helps you become more godly. It's not about judging each other. It's about loving each other enough to stay in each other's face. Spend some more time praying throughout the day about someone you think you would like to invite into your life to keep you accountable.

"Paul said, 'It has always been my ambition to preach the gospel where Christ was not known' (Rom. 15:20 NIV). What's your ambition?"

DAY 3

YOUR CLOSEST FRIENDS MUST BE ON FIRE FOR GOD

---

2 Corinthians 6:14–15

Do not be unequally yoked together with unbelievers. For what fellowship has righteousness with lawlessness? And what communion has light with darkness? And what accord has Christ with Belial? Or what part has a believer with an unbeliever?

As you get serious about really changing the world, you're going to have to limit the amount of time you spend with people who are of the world. The most important reason for you to spend time with people who aren't saved is to help get them saved and let God change their lives.

You can strike up an accountability friendship only with someone who loves God with all his heart and who's going to hold you to the same thing. If you've been hanging around people who aren't saved, who don't love God with all of their hearts, or who are lukewarm, you may have to change friends. You may have to tell them you can't hang out with them anymore.

Some people say we need to witness to these people, we need to share the Lord with them. That's true, but you can't be out on a limb all by yourself trying to get them saved, hoping they'll get saved so you'll have Christian friends. You've got to get locked in with people who are accountable to get in your face and push you toward the Lord.

> ## "Life is either a daring adventure or nothing."
> —Helen Keller

If you try to witness to your unsaved friends by yourself and hang out with them all the time, you just get weaker and weaker. They end up picking you off instead of your drawing them into the kingdom of God.

The Bible says in 2 Corinthians that we are not to be yoked together with non-Christians. In other words, don't hang out with them too much, don't be committed to them, don't let their ideas infiltrate your mind, and don't let them influence you.

Hang out with people who love God. They should be your closest friends. Join a pack of on-fire, blazing WorldChangers who will stay in your face about going for God with all of your heart. Then you can go out (maybe at school where there aren't many Christians around) and minister to other people with strength.

When your deep friendships are with people who really love God and are going after Him with all of their hearts, you don't have to depend on yourself alone to stay strong. You can draw strength from other people. You may go out all alone, but you go back to your pack of wild friends and tell them what's going on and how you're ministering. You witness to people of the world, but you don't draw them in and let them be your closest friends.

The Bible is very clear about the relationships Christians should have with unbelievers. It's not merely an issue of whether you should or shouldn't date them. The Bible is asking you to examine what you really have in common with them. How could you possibly think they could be your best friends when what's deepest in your heart is completely different from what's in their hearts?

Think about 2 Corinthians 6:14–15 today. Chew on it all day long. Memorize it, meditate on it, and think about any friendships you may need to cut off. Have you gotten so close to some unbelievers they've almost (or already) influenced you? You may need to cut off these unhealthy friendships this week.

Keep praying for the accountability friend(s) God is going to bring your way. He's going to use your accountability friendships to change your life.

CHALLENGE 4: Commit to an Accountability Friendship

DAY 4

PAUL'S FRIENDS

This accountability friendship idea is not just a casual suggestion; it's an absolute imperative. The devil has used this area for a long time to pick people off. Most people don't want to be honest with others. They want to cover everything up and pretend it's all right. They want to do everything alone. Then they wonder why they're backslidden and they feel so far away from God.

I'm not simply presenting a good suggestion that you'll follow only if it just happens without much effort on your part. Finding an accountability friend is absolute survival mode—you've got to do it if you're going to keep your fire. Let's look at the scriptural examples of Paul and Barnabas or Paul and Silas.

Paul went all over, traveling from village to village and town to town, starting churches, and ministering like crazy. He was an awesome, blazing man of God, but he never went by himself. He always had someone around him like Barnabas, Silas, or Timothy. Each man was in the other's face, pushing the other to go for God.

Now if anybody could stay strong and tight with God by himself, Paul should have been able to. However, Paul didn't trust himself to go alone. He knew an evil world was out there with way too many temptations to think that anyone could go it alone.

Yes, you have the power of God and the Word of God living inside you, but we all need outward motivation to keep our hearts and our minds focused. Paul took other people with him to help keep his heart and his mind focused.

It's funny how much less temptation you're drawn into when other people are around. You would never even think about certain sins with other people around you.

Take some time today and meditate on these friendship Scriptures we've been talking about this week. Then list two or three people, no more than that, who you think could really be an accountability friend like Paul had with Barnabas or Silas.

1. _____

2. _____

3. _____

Begin to pray that God will put the same thing on their hearts and see if God makes a divine connection just like He did with Paul and Barnabas.

DAY 5

IN-YOUR-FACE FRIENDSHIPS

Proverbs 27:6
You can trust a friend who corrects you (CEV).

🕐 Take a few minutes to memorize this verse before you go on today.

Accountability friendship is about being willing to get in each other's face. This is not saying, "Well, I'll pray for you, brother." Some of your Christian friends may be involved in the Christian cliché where they act like everything is all right, but inside they're not at all. They spend so much time playing sports or video games or doing other activities that they don't feel very close to anybody else anyway. There are people they say they're close to, but it's just because they go to the same youth group and sing "friends are friends forever" and have goose bumps together. But they don't really know each other. Accountability friendships are different.

Accountability friendships say, "I'm going to get in your face, and I'm going to let you get in my face. If you see anything in my life that doesn't line up with the Word of God, I expect you to call me on it." I call them *in-your-face friendships*.

In these friendships, you give someone permission to hold you accountable, to ask you how your quiet time was, what God spoke to you, and what's going on in your life. If you say, "Well, nothing really," then your accountability friend gets in your face and says, "Wait just a minute! Aren't you growing in the Lord? Don't you want to change the world?" Your account-ability partner gets in your face and says, "Listen, I will not stand for this. I love you too much to let you halfheartedly go through your quiet times and coast through your life."

Think back about the times somebody has gotten in your face and kept you from really making a big mistake. That is what accountability friendships are about. These are people you allow to get in your face—not because they have to but because you want them to. They help keep you from making big mistakes.

Write down a few areas you wish someone would get in your face about.

_____

_____

_____

One sign of real maturity is allowing one of your parents to be an accountability partner. Basically, you tell your mom and dad (or just choose one) that you want to give them permission to get in your face whenever they think they need to. They may get in your face anyway, but you're giving them permission to get in your face about anything they see in you that doesn't look like something in Jesus' life.

What would your parents do if you said that to them? They would probably fall over and faint for about a month. It is a true sign of maturity when you want your mom and dad to push you to grow in the things of the Lord.

Keep praying over those people you listed yesterday who God might want to use in your life to be an accountability friend to you.

DAY 6

WHAT TO TALK ABOUT WITH AN ACCOUNTABILITY FRIEND

John 15:15

No longer do I call you servants, for a servant does not know what his master is doing; but I have called you friends, for all things that I heard from My Father I have made known to you.

This is Jesus' definition of *friendship:* "Things that I heard My Father speak in private I've made known to you. I've told you about them. I've told you the deepest things in My heart that I wouldn't tell anyone else about. Now you're qualified to be My friend."

These accountability friendships you're developing should be with people with whom you are committed to sharing your heart, the very deepest part of yourself. Two or three people should really know everything about you—your deepest fears, desires, and longings. These are not people with whom you should ever allow yourself to be fake. Jesus said, "In order for you to be qualified to be My friends, you have to hear the deepest things of My life."

If you want people to really pray for you, you've got to tell them the most important prayer matters in your life. Don't just ask them to pray for you on the surface. Start sharing your very gut with them, and let them seriously pray for you about things that really matter. It's not, "Pray for me because I have a test in school this week." Pray for each other about a friendship at school, your parents, not feeling secure about yourself, or whatever you are going through that is really affecting who you are.

When you do that, you allow somebody the privilege of coming into your life. Then he can really be a true friend to you because he knows what is going on, and he can really care about you.

Accountability friendships allow you to develop the kinds of friendships that can end up changing the world, the kinds of friendships where you connect heart to heart and soul to soul. You guys are actually hooked together. It's not some surface "Christian" friendship, but you are people who really care about each other. You share your hearts on an ongoing basis and hold each other accountable to keep pressing toward the Lord.

Take some time and list some things here that you've wanted to share with other people but you've never found someone who cared enough to really listen.

There is going to be a time when God will give you some friends with whom you can really share these deep things from your heart. Keep asking. He has promised to hear you and answer.

DAY 7

BE FRIENDLY

Proverbs 18:24
A man who has friends must himself be friendly,
But there is a friend who sticks closer than a brother.

If you're going to have friends, you have to be friendly.

How do you find an accountability friendship? You don't find it by staying in a corner somewhere and hoping that God will bring someone to you. God will bring someone into your life, but you've got to get out there and show yourself friendly.

You've got to show that you want to be this kind of friend to somebody else. You're not just looking for somebody to wait on you and listen to you. You've got to be willing to wait on him, listen to him, and serve him.

You've got to show that you're interested in somebody else's life if you want somebody else to be interested in your life and help push you toward the Lord. You need to be like a heat-seeking missile going after the right kind of friend. Don't settle for whatever kind of people are in your path at school or your youth group.

Think about the kind of person you want for an accountability partner. She should be somebody you look up to. You see stuff in her life that looks like Jesus, and you want it in your life.

Look for somebody you want to be around because you know that his character will rub off on you. Find someone with wisdom to speak into your life.

It doesn't have to be an older person, just someone you admire because you see God in his life. Because your friendship will be incredibly deep and you will share some very personal secrets, it would be a good idea for this person to be the same sex as you.

Continue to pray for your new friend now, and ask God to begin to mold her heart and draw her toward you as an accountability friend, as you've already been doing this week. Begin to be friendly now; show yourself friendly to her.

Don't dump this heavy accountability thing on a person right away. Talk to him about what is going on in his heart and see what you can pray with him about. Later, you can talk to him about being accountable to each other. Say something like, "Listen, I want you to get in my face about stuff. Maybe we could get in each other's face and really push each other toward the Lord."

Now is your chance to go for it. Don't just sit there thinking about it anymore. Don't wait for someone to come up to you and ask you to be her accountability partner. You're going to have to go after it. It's not an option. It's not just a good idea. It's something you're going to have to relentlessly pursue.

Are you only thirteen or fifteen years old? Whatever your age, you're not too young to have an accountability partner who stays in your face. Somebody who is going to change the world has got to be hooked in with other people. Your closest friends should be people who are blazing maniacs and who want to change the world just like you do.

Now commit to go out and begin to talk to the people you've been praying about all week. Talk to them and pursue accountability friendships in a very specific way. Decide right now what you plan to do in this accountability friendship this week. God bless you. You can change the world!

I commit to be a WorldChanger and to surround myself with at least two or three accountable friends who will help push me toward the Lord. I will stay connected with accountable friends all through my teen years. They can stay in my face, and I will stay in their faces so that by the time I am twenty I will have developed solid friendships that have pushed me to become all that I can be as a WorldChanger.

_____   _____
WorldChanger's Signature   Date

Week 2

CHALLENGE 5:
Commit to a Lifestyle of Worship and Holy Actions

DAY 1

BECOME A LIVING SACRIFICE

Romans 12:1

Therefore, I urge you, brothers, in view of God's mercy, to offer your bodies as living sacrifices, holy and pleasing to God—this is your spiritual act of worship (NIV).

Paul encourages, exhorts, and commands us to present our bodies as living sacrifices so that what we do will be an acceptable means of worship to God. In other words, we can worship with our lips, but God wants us to worship with our very lives.

The way we live should be an expression of worship to the Lord. He wants us to be holy, pure, and acceptable to Him. The Bible tells us to take our bodies and, instead of offering them to the world, offer them as living sacrifices to God.

Romans 6:13

Do not offer the parts of your body to sin, as instruments of wickedness, but rather offer yourselves to God, as those who have been brought from death to life; and offer the parts of your body to him as instruments of righteousness (NIV).

God wants us to live a holy lifestyle so that when people look at us, they say, "Wow! You look like Jesus, like nothing I've ever seen before."

Paul urges us to make sure that how we live lines up with what we say that we believe. Make sure that your words are not just a bunch of hot air coming out of your lips but that they are coming out of your life. The things you do and say should reflect what you believe. What you say you believe should be evident in the way you live.

James 2:18 says, "Show me your faith without your works, and I will show you my faith by my works." James is saying, "You can see that I have faith because the way that I am living reflects that what I believe has really taken hold in my life."

As a WorldChanger, you have to refuse to let the worldly habits you see around you dominate your life. Although you have to live in this world, you don't have to be like the world. You can see through the games that the world plays, and you are smarter than that; you can live above it. You are called to live a lifestyle of worship that refuses to allow any habits from the world to creep into your life.

What do you think it means to present yourself as a living sacrifice? Write your definition here.

_____

_____

_____

To sacrifice something is to completely give it away. In the Old Testament, when the priests sacrificed a lamb, they would actually kill it and present it to the Lord. Compare this to offering yourself as a living sacrifice. Although you don't actually die, you completely and totally give yourself over to the Lord. You present yourself to Him, saying, "Lord, use me. Use my life while I've still got breath in me to show this world what You really look like."

Take some time to meditate on Romans 6:13. Think about what you can do to present yourself as a living sacrifice and to fully give yourself over to the Lord today. Take some time right now to write out a few of these ideas here.

Now go out and do these things today.

CHALLENGE 5: Commit to a Lifestyle of Worship and Holy Actions

DAY 2

FOR THE GLORY OF GOD

Colossians 3:17

    And whatever you do in word or deed, do all in the name of the Lord Jesus, giving thanks to God the Father through Him.

1 Corinthians 10:31

    Therefore, whether you eat or drink, or whatever you do, do all to the glory of God.

God is concerned about all the things we do, even about our eating or drinking. We need to do everything in the name of the Lord; everything we do should give Him glory. He looks at our lives as through a microscope, and He wants to be glorified in everything we do and everything we say.

You can't allow yourself to think that the only time God sees your life is when you're at church or youth group. You can't think that God looks only at certain parts of your life and not all of it. He wants every bit of your life to give Him glory. He wants you to be like a mirror. When people look at you, they should see a reflection of what He looks like.

You have to love God more than you love your old sinful habits. You have to love God more than you love secular music, cars, clothes, or friends. You have to love God more than the little bit of fun you sometimes believe sin may present. You need to be drawn to God rather than to the world.

If you are determined that the things you do should be as worship to Him, then you need to stay in His presence all day long. Psalm 22:3 says that God inhabits the praises of His people. That means when you really praise and worship God, He hangs out with you all day long.

When you purpose in your heart to live holy and pure before Him, you can begin to stay in His presence all day long. The moment you think a sinful thought, you can sense things start to go wrong all around you. God can't hang out where there is sin.

The most awesome thing about the Christian life is that as you stay holy and pure, God's presence is available to you! He'll open up the door of your heart and cause things to happen to benefit you and put your life back together.

As a WorldChanger, you need to make a decision that whatever you do, you are going to bring God glory. You want people to look at your life and realize how awesome God is because of what they see.

Write out a couple of things that you have done in your life that portray Jesus well.

```
┌─────────────────────────────────────────────────────────┐
│  ✏                                                        │
│                                                           │
│   _____     │
│                                                           │
│   _____     │
│                                                           │
└─────────────────────────────────────────────────────────┘
```

Write out a couple of things you could do today to portray Jesus in your life.

```
┌─────────────────────────────────────────────────────────┐
│  ✏                                                        │
│                                                           │
│   _____     │
│                                                           │
│   _____     │
│                                                           │
└─────────────────────────────────────────────────────────┘
```

Memorize 1 Corinthians 10:31; chew on it all day. Decide right now that everything you do will bring glory to God each day.

CHALLENGE 5: Commit to a Lifestyle of Worship and Holy Actions

DAY 3

NO VILE THING

Psalm 101:3
I will set before my eyes
*   no vile thing.*
The deeds of faithless men I hate;
*   they will not cling to me (NIV).*

Something is wicked when it is so offensive to the senses that you can't even stand it. It's repulsive. David says here, "I'm not

going to put anything in front of my face that looks disgusting."
It was a decision he was making to stay in a worshipful lifestyle.
He refused to set in front of himself anything that was vile to
God.

This is the commitment of a WorldChanger. It says, "I refuse
to even accidentally allow any vile, disgusting thing in my life."
This would include drugs, drinking, immorality, perversion, TV,
movies, magazines, anything that leads to a sinful lifestyle or a
sinful way of thinking.

Take a moment now and list some vile or evil things that,
in the usual course of your day, are easy to be exposed to
whether at school or work.

I want you to make a decision today to set no vile thing before
your eyes. Make a commitment not to pay attention to it. Turn your
head when it tries to get your attention.

Take this verse in Psalm 101, and meditate on it all day long.
Go for it like a WorldChanger, and win in this area of your life
today.

DAY 4

MAKE A RADICAL COMMITMENT

---

1 Corinthians 10:23

"Everything is permissible"—but not everything is benefi-cial. "Everything is permissible"—but not everything is con-structive (NIV).

When you commit your heart and life to Christ, there are a lot of things you could do but not everything will be in your best interest. As a young man or woman of God who is determined to be a WorldChanger, you've got to decide what things you will refuse to let be a part of your life because they're not beneficial.

Just by going through this WorldChanger Bible study, you are expressing a desire to change the world, live for God, and be a ballistic Christian. Now is the time to choose to do the things you know will help you get where you want to go. There are things you could do that are not totally sin, but they're not going to take you where you want to go. You would end up on a treadmill going nowhere fast.

A lot of people say you can watch a certain movie because there's only one bad part, or it's all right to listen to some music because the language isn't really that bad. However, as a Christian who wants to change the world, you need to say, "Yeah, I probably could do that, but there is some stuff I don't want inside me because it's not beneficial and it's not going to help me grow or change the world. I'm not a Christian who just wants to make it to heaven. I want to put my foot down and change my school and change the world, and I've got to start right now. I could get away with some of these things and still be a Christian and go to heaven, but that's not good enough for me. I want to change the world on my way to heaven."

Galatians 5:13

You, my brothers, were called to be free. But do not use your freedom to indulge the sinful nature; rather, serve one another in love (NIV).

Just because you're free, don't use your freedom to get caught up in the sinful nature. Before you know it, you are once again a slave to sin, the very thing from which Jesus has redeemed you.

You may need to make some radical commitments. For example, you may want to choose not to see R-rated movies or not to listen to secular music. Make these commitments with your whole heart. Don't long for the things of the world.

Right now is the time to make a decision not to get involved in any of the vile things into which the world would draw you. I want you to take a little time and write out some things you commit not to do anymore. You should make this commitment because you know that these things are vile and pulling you into a way of thinking that will not help you become a World-Changer.

Take five minutes and memorize 1 Corinthians 10:23 right now. Meditate on it all day today.

Think about the things that would be permissible but not beneficial for you to do. Being specific, write out some of those things now.

_____

_____

_____

Now make a decision that even though you are permitted to do these things, you will refuse to do them because you are going to be a Christian who is set aside by God to really make a difference and change this world.

CHALLENGE 5: Commit to a Lifestyle of Worship and Holy Actions

DAY 5

NO IDOLS

If you're going to be a person who will change this world, you can't have any idols in your life. What is an idol? An idol is anything you love more than you love God. Your idol could be a person, or it could be an object. You don't usually intend to make somebody or something an idol. You just begin liking it more and more, and pretty soon you love it more than you love God. You can tell by how much time you spend with the object of your affections, how much you think about it, and what you are willing to do for it. Somebody with a lifestyle of worship purposes in his heart to worship only God.

There is only one proper thing to do with an idol in your life, and this process is described in Exodus 32:20. The story is about the golden calf that the Israelites built. Everyone was worshiping and bowing down to this false god when Moses came off the mountain. Consider the idols in your life. Try to think of what they have ever really done for you. You may think they have done a lot, just like the Israelites thought their cow had delivered them from Egypt.

This Scripture describes exactly what Moses did with that idol.

Exodus 32:20
Then he took the calf which they had made, burned it in the fire, and ground it to powder; and he scattered it on the water and made the children of Israel drink it.

Now that's drastic action. He said, "We're going to obliterate this idol so that you will never have the chance to worship this vile thing again." That is exactly what you and I need to do when we find idols creeping into our lives. We need to absolutely destroy them. In your life, it could mean not renting R-rated movies. It could mean throwing away secular tapes or getting rid of materialistic thinking. Or it could mean ending a relationship you have begun to value more than your relationship with God.

You need to get rid of an idol so that there is no way you could *ever* worship it again. I know this sounds like pretty drastic action, but it is so freeing when you absolutely rip the idols out of your life. I've seen thousands of teenagers make commitments to get rid of secular music. They've sent letters and pictures of themselves destroying their music and describing how free they finally are in Christ. They talk about having chains around their necks and trying to live for God but always falling away. When they made a decision to crush their idols, they had great freedom and finally were able to start blazing for God like they wanted to do.

I want you to list a few idols in your life that you need to obliterate.

Make a commitment today to do as Moses did with the calf and rip these vile things out of your life. Trash them today and see how much freedom God will give you in exchange.

DAY 6

THE VALUE OF A WORSHIPFUL LIFESTYLE

Why is it so important to have a worshipful lifestyle? Basically, worshiping God is bowing down before His throne and acknowledging His awesomeness. The only way He allows you to come before His throne is for you to remove all the junk from your life. You don't have to be perfect; you just have to be humble and admit to the Lord where you've blown it and then do everything possible to rid your life of the idols. Quote Scripture, rip the bad stuff out of your life, and live completely holy before Him.

"Missions is . . . 'getting out of your comfort zone.'"

—Wendy

The most awesome thing you can know is that your life is completely right and holy. When you have a clear conscience before God, He blows your face off, and His presence comes down and hovers over you all day and all night. You are living your life before the throne of God. You're into God and He's into you; you're speaking to Him and He's speaking to you.

Matthew 5:24

Leave your gift there before the altar, and go your way. First be reconciled to your brother, and then come and offer your gift.

Jesus talked about offering a gift of sacrifice to the Lord. When you have something in your heart against somebody, you should leave your gift, go, and make things right before you come back. You can't expect to come completely before the Lord in worship if something is not right in your life or heart. Whether it is between you and another person or between you and God, you've got to make things right first.

If you want God to use you to change the world, you've got to make sure everything in your life is pure and holy so that He can walk with you all day long and you can feel His incredible presence.

Take a minute now to write down anything that might be standing in your way of an awesome time of worshiping God.

_____

_____

_____

Commit to make things right so you can walk in holiness and purity before God today.

DAY 7

A HIGHER STANDARD

We've been talking about your living a lifestyle of worship with no vile thing in your life. That means living a life in which people look at you and see a reflection of Jesus. Whatever you say and do is incredibly pure.

Practically speaking, what should you do about the things in your life? Begin to look at all your habits. The way you talk, the way you act, the way you use your spare time, the way you think—all are important. Now ask yourself how they compare to Scripture.

How does the way you're talking and living compare to Scripture? How does it compare to what Jesus or other people of the Bible thought was important? What does God have to say about these areas?

As a WorldChanger, you are going to have to say no to some things to which other people, maybe even other Christians, would say yes. Your desire to change the world does not permit you to do things other Christians might get away with or feel like they could do. Your seriousness and focus demand a higher level of living and caliber of intensity. You don't do what comes naturally; you measure everything by the Word of God. You refuse to allow yourself to give in to the usual way of living because you have a higher standard and a higher calling. Your whole youth group might be doing it, everyone might be saying it's okay, but that doesn't matter. You have made a radical commitment to rub every piece of vile activity out of your life because you love God more than you love the world.

Today, I want you to take the Scriptures you've been memorizing this week and chew on them all day. I want you to make the commitment of a WorldChanger who demands holiness and purity of yourself. As soon as you detect sin in your life, be committed to get it out and allow no vile thing to stand before you.

"Missions is . . . 'letting God use us in our weakness as we're giving them our precious gift.'"

—Alisa

I commit to live a lifestyle of worship so that in everything I say and do I give God glory. I commit to put no vile thing before my eyes. I refuse to allow any influences of the world that would draw me away from God into my life. No matter what the cost or how much other people say these things are okay, my commitment is to change the world. To do that, I've got to be absolutely pure in everything I say and do.

_____   _____
WorldChanger's Signature   Date

WEEK 8

CHALLENGE 6:
Commit to Holy Courtship Instead of Dating

DAY 1

THE WORLD'S DATING SYSTEM

Philippians 4:19
And my God shall supply all your need according to His riches in glory by Christ Jesus.

Take three minutes and memorize this verse.

WorldChangers can see through the games the world throws at them, including the dating scene games. The modern dating scene is designed to make you feel stupid or weird if you don't have a date. It makes you feel that you have to have somebody to love on you or have on your shoulder or have your arm around in order to be worth anything. You feel like a social misfit if you don't have someone to go out with.

The modern dating game is a game of going out with who looks the cutest or who looks the toughest. You are so busy trying to be what you think the other person wants, you are really never yourself. You really don't know if the person likes you or not because you have been fake with each other the whole time.

It's a game of looking "cutesy, cutesy" all the time and wondering what so-and-so is saying about so-and-so and I like this guy/this girl and he is saying such and such about so-and-so and she wants to date someone else but he's mad at her because she . . . It's just a big game that totally distracts you from what God really wants to do in you and through you.

This whole teenage love thing totally rips people out of their walk with God. They get so distracted by some guy or girl who

mesmerizes them that they forget they really should be seeking God and not another person.

I have talked to many young people who have compromised their Christian walk by allowing themselves to get into the situation described above. The Bible talks about loving the Lord our God with all of the heart, soul, and mind (Matt. 22:37). Your desire for Him needs to be stronger than your desire for a date, stronger than your desire for a girlfriend or boyfriend, and the acceptance you think you might get from that. Many times you probably think, *I need to have a boyfriend (or girlfriend); I need to be loved by somebody*. Let me tell you, God knows what you need. The problem is this: if you think you need somebody, you're not ready for anybody. Your need for love and acceptance cannot be met by another person; it can be met only by God.

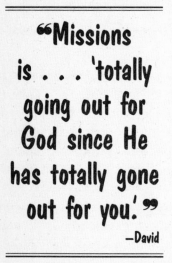

"Missions is . . . 'totally going out for God since He has totally gone out for you.'"

—David

Today's verse says that God will supply all your needs. God knows what you need—He made you. He knows what you're made of, and He knows how to meet your needs. You don't need a boyfriend or girlfriend. You need a relationship with Jesus. You need to be tied up in God more than you ever have been in your life. The Bible says that He knows your needs. As you are hooked up in Him, He will meet these needs. So if you feel as if you need another person, you really need to quote and chew on this verse all day long. Trust that God will do what He says because He never lies. He promised, "I will meet every one of your needs."

I know that this sounds radical, and it sounds drastic, but if you are going to change the world, then you are going to have to see through this game. It will only pull you down and suck the life out of you. You will soon forget the fire you once had. Take Philippians 4:19 and chew on it today, anytime you feel you have a need. Concentrate on this Scripture especially if you feel you need a girlfriend or boyfriend. I want you to take this verse and cram it down your throat and have confidence that God will supply your need.

CHALLENGE 6: Commit to Holy Courtship Instead of Dating

DAY 2

COURTSHIP VERSUS DATING

Developing a courting relationship is completely different from developing a dating relationship. I want you to develop a level of maturity that allows you to see through all the games the world throws at you. The first thing you have to do is to back away from the modern dating game and commit to go after God with all your heart. Then find healthy ways to develop a friendship. This friendship may or may not lead to a romantic relationship, but the friendship should be your first priority. Don't just jump from one relationship to another depending solely on who's available at the time. That's a sickening game, and you have to be smarter than that.

Be confident that God will supply all your needs. Choose to back away from any kind of dating relationship and go full blast into God. Find out some courtship principles from the Scripture. You will be able to use them to develop a wholesome relationship that will ultimately lead to marriage.

Proverbs 14:8
The wisdom of the prudent is to give thought to their ways,
  but the folly of fools is deception (NIV).

Proverbs 14:15
A simple man believes anything,
  but a prudent man gives thought to his steps (NIV).

The point being made here is that if you're going to be wise, you need to give thought to your ways and thought to your steps. Don't be sucked into this dating thing. You need to think about what you're doing before you do it. Don't just date because everyone else does. Just because everyone else kisses on the first date or on the third date or everybody else gets into some kind of sexual activity doesn't mean you should. You have to think about your ways.

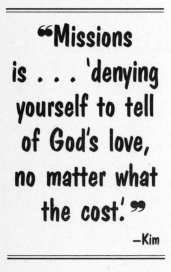

"Missions is . . . 'denying yourself to tell of God's love, no matter what the cost.'"

—Kim

Your ways are your actions. It's the way you flirt, the way you wink or smile, the way you flip your hair for a guy or flex your muscles when you walk by a girl. Think about the things you do that attract or lure people because of your desire for attention. Remember, God will supply all your needs. You don't need a guy or a girl checking you out every time you walk by to feel as if you're worth something. God says you're worth a lot because He made you. He says you're beautifully and wonderfully made. You're awesome, man. He put you together and made you an incredible young man or woman of God.

Think about what you do and why you do it. Give thought to your ways. If you love the Lord with all your heart, put no vile thing before your eyes. You don't want to look like the world in any way. When you think about what you do before you do it, it begins to change the way you do things. Don't just do what they do on some TV show and think that it's okay because everybody does it—it isn't okay and everyone isn't doing it. WorldChangers, wise young men and women, are giving thought to their steps. Before you do something, before you ask somebody out, before you continue in the typical dating lifestyle, think about it.

> "Missions is . . . 'a lifestyle, not some place you go.'"
> —Jennifer

In the accountability chapter, we discussed principles regarding how to proceed with a friendship. You can apply these directly to a court-ship relationship as well. In a court-ship, you think through all the ramifications of a relationship. You're not pulled into anything since you're thinking about where the relationship is going. Ask yourself some serious questions: Am I really pursuing God? Is this relationship going to help me become a WorldChanger? Is something distracting me from my relationship with God? Am I letting this person become an idol in my life? If you honestly answered all these questions in the right way, then you are giving thought to your ways.

Considering what you know about not letting vile thoughts or distractions get in your way, what can you take from your account-ability friendships and apply to a courtship relationship? Use the principles to begin to walk down the road to a friendship that could lead to a romance. That is what courtship is about: using godly principles to build a friendship that could lead to a romance and, ultimately, to marriage. Now *that* is different from the American dating scene.

Take a few moments and list here what you think the advantages are of courtship versus the American dating scene.

1. _____

2. _____

3. _____

4. _____

Take these two Scriptures—Proverbs 14:8, 15—with you all day long. Think about what things you might be doing that you should consider more carefully before you continue to do them. In fact, take a few moments and list some things you have done or are doing that you might need to think through seriously before you continue. They could include the way you have looked at guys or girls or approached them and flirted with them, anything in the way you handle yourself around members of the opposite sex.

1. _____

2. _____

3. _____

4. _____

It is time to change the dating scene. Let it start with you today.

DAY 3

FRIENDSHIP BEFORE COURTSHIP

You must determine to have a friendship before a courtship relationship if you and the other person want to really know each other. It's amazing to me how people can sit by each other in a class and a week later they are dating and a week after that they are having a sexual relationship. They really don't know each other. They say it's love at first sight, but I don't think they even know the definition of love. They figure it's okay to go out and get involved if they are in love.

The Bible says in Colossians 3:1–2: "Since, then, you have been raised with Christ, set your hearts on things above, where Christ is seated at the right hand of God. Set your minds on things above, not on earthly things" (NIV).

You memorized that Scripture a few weeks ago, and I want you to understand what it means. You should be in control of where your heart goes. You choose to set your heart on the things above and not on the things of the earth. I want to share something with you that you may find hard to believe: this whole concept of falling in love is not in the Bible. It really is nothing more than infatuation. Some people try to make a distinction between being infatuated and falling in love, but there is no difference the way we use the words in our society.

The dictionary's definition of *infatuation* is "to make foolish, to deprive of sound judgment, to inspire with a foolish or shallow love or affection" (*Webster's New World Dictionary, Third Collegiate Edition*). In other words, when someone is infatuated, he looks like a fool because he is doing something without using sound judgment.

The very expression, "falling in love," implies a lack of control. "I don't know, man. It was the weirdest thing. I was just walking along, minding my own business, when all of a sudden I fell down. Then BOOM! There I was—in love!" The Bible says that we don't fall or trip into anything. We aren't pulled into anything beyond our will. Don't be like a big, gaping satellite dish, wide open to any love signals that might fly your way. You're smarter than that. Guard your heart.

The trouble is that this concept of falling in love has been around for so long, even your parents sometimes encourage it. They'll say things like, "You're in love, aren't you?" You think, *Well, I guess I am. Should I be? I don't know. Maybe I'm weird if I'm not.* Just because your parents use these words or are familiar with the concept doesn't mean it is holy and godly. Most young people are doing what they have seen other people do. We know that love is from God, so isn't falling in love from God, too? Wrong. This is infatuation.

> **"Missions is . . . 'giving of yourself to the people of other parts of the world and totally being blown away with the results!'"**
>
> —Kristy

The kind of love God has for you has nothing to do with falling. He doesn't want you falling into anything because you'll just fall back out again. You aren't a feeble little thing who falls into a hole. That is not what God created you for. God created you as a man or woman with destiny, focus, and purpose. He created you to take wise steps according to His wisdom that will lead you to a fulfilled and happy lifestyle. If you fall into anything, including love, it will not lead to your benefit in the long run.

It's time to think about what it means to set your heart on the things above. If you set your heart and mind on things above, then you will not get tripped up into this falling-in-love thing, and you will make a decision to have wholesome friendships. I recommend a prerequisite to a courtship relationship. Make sure you two have been in a healthy friendship for at least a year before you consider romance and that your accountability friend knows what is going on with the potential romance.

Take Colossians 3:1–2 and chew on it all day. Concentrate on setting your heart on things above. Don't get lured into the things of this world.

CHALLENGE 6: Commit to Holy Courtship Instead of Dating

DAY 4

FLEE FROM IMMORALITY

---

1 Corinthians 6:18–20

Flee sexual immorality. Every sin that a man does is outside the body, but he who commits sexual immorality sins against his own body. Or do you not know that your body is the temple of the Holy Spirit who is in you, whom you have from God, and you are not your own? For you were bought at a price; therefore glorify God in your body.

As you begin to walk down the road toward having a holy courtship that is a pure relationship, it is imperative for you to recognize that the devil will try to mess you up physically. Even if you obey all the principles of having a friendship first and accountability in your life, the devil can still entice you into sexual immorality as you walk toward a courtship.

The Bible says to flee immorality. Your body is the temple of the Holy Spirit. In other words, God lives inside you. Don't take this thing that God lives inside and use it for anything impure.

God is looking for a generation of young people who have decided that they are going to protect their hearts, their minds, and their bodies. They are not just going to say no to intercourse. They are going to say no to petting and to any kind of sexual involvement whatsoever. I have heard the testimonies of young people who have made the commitment not to have sex.

"Missions is . . . 'reaching out to people who are lost and dying.'"

—Dave

You may have heard of the True Love Waits rallies that allow you to plant your written commitment in the ground in Washington, D.C. I wholeheartedly agree with this idea of making a commitment to stay pure and not have sex until the day you marry. If you have already been involved sexually, then make a fresh commitment to stay pure and never do it again until you're married. It's sort of like a second virginity. Once you get the revelation, the lights come on and you say, "Man, I'm going to keep my body pure until the day I'm married." If you have never had sex, then great; never have it while you're unmarried.

There have been cases of young ladies getting pregnant even though they have never had sex. What? How could that happen? They did not have intercourse, but they were fooling around enough that semen from the male was able to get inside them and they got pregnant. It isn't enough to commit to not having the act of sex. You must absolutely stay away from any situation where you even come close. The point is that some people think they are staying pure just because they do not have sexual intercourse. This is not about, "How close can I come without getting caught or pregnant?" It is about living with a pure heart so that you do not even fool around with sexual impropriety. It is about honoring the Word of God so much and respecting that other person so much that you would not dare lay a hand on him or her in a sexual way until you are married. A great way to live up to that high standard is to stay around a lot of accountability friends and to keep the lights on wherever you are. If the lights are on and friends are around, then it is hard to mess up.

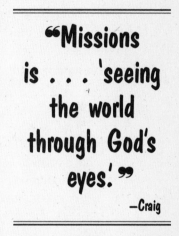

"Missions is . . . 'seeing the world through God's eyes.'"

—Craig

God is looking for World-Changers who are radically, passionately committed to every part of their lives being totally clean. This is the time to commit your body, every part of it, to purity. Decide that you will not allow anyone to touch you or fondle you in any way, including sexual intercourse. Until you find the one who is committed to be with you forever and you actually have the ceremony in front of a preacher and a whole crowd, never allow anyone to touch you.

I want you to memorize 1 Corinthians 6:18–20 today. Chew on it, chew on it, and chew on it all day long.

Day 5

FLEE FROM IMPURITY

It is imperative in a courtship relationship to say no to impurity. I want to emphasize this one more day because you're going to face these temptations and you're going to have to know what to do. The story of Joseph is a great example.

Genesis 39:6–12

Now Joseph was well-built and handsome, and after a while his master's wife took notice of Joseph and said, "Come to bed with me!" But he refused. "With me in charge," he told her, "my master does not concern himself with anything in the house; everything he owns he has entrusted to my care. No one is greater in this house than I am. My master has withheld nothing from me except you, because you are his wife. How then could I do such a wicked thing and sin against God?" And though she spoke to Joseph day after day, he refused to go to bed with her or even be with her. One day he went into the house to attend to his duties, and none of the household servants was inside. She caught him by his cloak and said, "Come to bed with me!" But he left his cloak in her hand and ran out of the house (NIV).

You know this story. Joseph finds himself alone in the house with his master's wife. She wants him to have sex with her. This young man is in a situation where no one probably would have ever found out what he had done, but he has the fire and courage to say no. You will probably find yourself in a similar situation at some point in your life. The devil will try to trick you into thinking that no one will ever find out. That is the time when you have to have the boldness to say, "Man, even if no one finds out about this, I cannot sin against my God like this. I cannot sin against my own body. God lives inside me. I will not use this temple of the Holy Spirit for evil." That is the time for you to flee. The time to make the commitment to flee is right now before you ever get in that situation. When you start feeling the temptation, the only proper response is to scream NO! as loud as you can and then run the other direction.

I have talked to so many young couples, even those who loved the Lord, who got into a tempting situation and gave in. Each one wished that the other had screamed NO! But neither one did, and they were lured into something unholy. You need to make the commitment right now to say no. Then when the proper time comes, when God says you're ready for a courtship, you need to discuss this issue right up front. Say, "Listen, if anything ever happens, I want you to have the guts to say no. If any kind of temptation comes up, let's protect ourselves from it now. Let's make sure we don't get in the dark or spend time alone with each other. If anything does ever come up, I want to tell you right now, be bold." Say, "I want to be just like Joseph. I'm going to say no and run the other way. We will not be lured into an unholy situation, and that is just the way it is."

> **"Missions is . . . 'taking time to minister to others.'"**
>
> —Peter

If you get used to saying no now, then you will be able to say no all the way through your life. When you get married, you will want to marry someone who also knows how to say no. There will be temptation throughout your life. You have to practice saying no right now because the devil will try to get in your face the rest of your life. He will try to lure you away from your spouse.

You need to start practicing now to say no with all your heart and flee and run the other direction, and you want to proceed in a courtship only with somebody you know will say no. You don't want to marry somebody and always wonder how your spouse would respond to temptation given the opportunity. You want to have the confidence of knowing that no matter what, your spouse would say no and run the other way. You want to give your spouse that same confidence in you.

DAY 6

CHALLENGE 6: Commit to Holy Courtship Instead of Dating

GUARD YOUR HEART

Proverbs 4:23
Above all else, guard your heart,
for it is the wellspring of life (NIV).

This whole idea of pursuing a courtship when God says it is right versus having a modern-day dating relationship has to do with guarding your heart. Your heart is one of the most precious parts of your being. If you let any old person come into your heart and lure you into a relationship, then your heart is going to get busted up, ripped apart, broken up, and stomped on. It is obvious all around you. You can look around at the people in your school and see how many are hurt because someone let them down, how many have had their emotions crushed, or how many girls have gotten pregnant. We're talking about not falling in love and just letting your lips fly onto anyone who comes your way. Letting a boy put his arm around you or a girl hang on your shoulder just because that person looks halfway cool or popular is *bogus*.

You have to guard your heart. You have to protect it from getting crushed and smashed. Out of your heart comes the wellspring of life. It is the very center of your life, your joy and zest for living. You can't walk through life like most people do. Their hearts have been beaten up and stabbed, and walked on and stabbed, and walked on and walked on. One day you may want to get married. If you have given your heart to anyone you ever went on a date with, what will make this person you want to marry so special?

Man, you have to guard your heart. When you give it away, you are giving away the remote control of your life. Just like someone could take the remote control for a car and run the car off a cliff or smash it into a wall, some people do that when you give them your heart. They smash you up and then laugh when you crash.

Guard your heart. Out of it comes the wellspring of life. But out of it can come misery if you let people walk on it and stab it. You have to guard it, protect it, and set it on things above. Then when God has the right relationship for you, you can pursue a courtship. Continue to guard your heart until you have enough trust in the friendship that you know and have confidence that your heart will not be abused or misused.

Take some time to meditate on Proverbs 4:23, and think about what you can do to guard your heart. Write out two or three ways here.

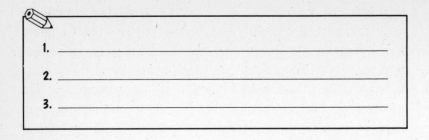

1. _____

2. _____

3. _____

DAY 7

CHALLENGE 6: Commit to Holy Courtship Instead of Dating

PRINCIPLES TO GUIDE YOUR RELATIONSHIP

We've been talking about how a WorldChanger doesn't get involved in a "falling in love" kind of dating but uses sound judgment in deciding what to do. I want to give some guiding principles for your relationship now. When the time is right for you to develop a courtship, you won't want to have gone through your teen years having had a dozen, six, or even a couple of dating relationships. I know Christians do it all over the place. Youth group members fall in love with each other, and it messes up the whole youth group. It's time for you to get smart.

WorldChangers have a different agenda. WorldChangers want to change the world. They're not just looking for someone to slap their lips on. They're not just looking for somebody to be the other half of a good-looking couple. They're looking at how they can change the world. If God brings the right person into their lives, they can change the world together. Let's talk about some principles you can use to guide a courtship.

What are some areas in your personal development that you would like to grow in before you get into a courtship? In other words, maybe there are some areas in your life where you are immature. Are there areas where you have been struggling with sin? Maybe you have some thought habits you have been struggling with. Are there Scriptures you have been wanting to memorize? We all have areas where we know we need to be stronger.

When you get into a real relationship, you don't want to give 25 percent or 50 percent of yourself. You don't want to be some old slob Christian who is barely hanging out with God. You want to be the very best that you can be when you give yourself to another person. You want to be full, whole, and developed in every area.

Think about the areas you want to develop before you would ever consider getting involved with a deep relationship. These areas could be habits you want to get over or sin you want to deal with in your life. Maybe you want more maturity in the way you think and the way you talk. List five or six of these areas here now.

1. _____

2. _____

3. _____

4. _____

5. _____

6. _____

Think about what you want to see developed in a guy or a girl before you start a courtship. Maybe you want to know that he has lived a constant Christian life for at least a year or two before you date him. You want to make sure she is not on the rebound from somebody else, and she only wants you now because she has to have somebody. Is he submissive to his parents? You should make sure that she has made a commitment to be a WorldChanger or to read through her Bible and seek the Lord. That would be a great prerequisite.

You don't want to date just anybody who takes a liking to you. When you have your heart and life together as a WorldChanger, a lot of people will find you attractive. You have to have high standards. Don't just consider if he is tall, dark, and handsome. Set standards for what his character is on the inside. You don't want somebody who has been throwing her lips all over every other guy in town and who is now sweet on you. The standards that you choose for a guy or a girl should be different from what people in the world choose. List five or six standards that you set for somebody you would enter into a courtship relationship with.

1. _____

2. _____

3. _____

4. _____

5. _____

6. _____

Think about how to proceed once you have grown to the point that you are ready and have met somebody you think is also ready for a courtship relationship. You need to set some guidelines now for what you want later (give thought to your ways). What do you want in your friendship with that person before you ever begin a courtship? Consider having an accountability friendship with that person for at least a year. You should know each other and be friends for at least a year before you would think of giving your heart away. Make sure that both of you are reading through the Scriptures. Make sure that both of you are committed to change the world. Commit together that both of you will have a Joseph attitude where you will scream and run from sexual immorality.

What do you want to do in your relationship to protect your fire and purity before God? Determine together to read the Bible or worship together for a specific amount of time each week. Don't lose your focus. Stay consumed with God, not each other. Don't go on dates every single night or even every weekend. Don't spend hours on the phone every day. Stay balanced. Keep your other friendships, those you had before you met as well as new ones you'll develop together.

List five or six guidelines or principles for how you will proceed in a courtship to be pure and holy in your relationship.

1. _____

2. _____

3. _____

4. _____

5. _____

6. _____

I commit to establish a courtship relationship and to avoid the typical dating relationship in whatever kind of romance I pursue. I commit to keep my body pure from sexual intercourse and any other kind of physical contact that would promote sexual indiscretion. I will keep my body pure because it is the temple of the Holy Spirit. I commit to live by the guidelines that I listed here and to keep my heart set on things above so I do not accidentally trip into falling in love and into the same dating game that the rest of my peers are in.

_____

WorldChanger's Signature

_____

Date

Week 9

CHALLENGE 7:
Commit to Honor
Your Parents

DAY 1

BE BLESSED

Ephesians 6:1–3

Children, obey your parents in the Lord, for this is right. "Honor your father and mother," which is the first commandment with promise: "that it may be well with you and you may live long on the earth."

Young people who have had anything to do with the Lord have heard this Scripture a thousand times, usually out of their parents' mouths. This is the Scripture that most young people wish wasn't even in the Bible because their parents use it against them so much. However, if you're going to be a WorldChanger, you have to be committed to living this Scripture even when you don't feel like it, even when it doesn't make sense. You have to be committed to honoring your mom and dad. The Bible says that if you honor them, you will live long and you will be blessed. If you honor them, God will put His anointing on everything you do, and it will all turn to gold and be successful.

Some people wonder, Why is everything going wrong in my life? Why does everything seem to fall down around me? Why does it seem like God's blessing is not on my life? Yet for other people, why does everything seem to go right? To answer these questions, you need to see if the blessing of God has been taken from your life.

First of all, have you given your life to the Lord? Are you living free from sin? Are you going after God and reading the Word with all your heart? Now, check, are you honoring your parents? God gives His word that if you honor your mother and father, things will go well with you.

A lot of people think that the more they can get away with, the better life they'll have. They think, *If I can just do this behind my parents' back and not get caught, then I'll have more fun.* The Bible says that just the opposite is true. It says that when you honor your parents, that's when things go well for you. That's when your life is pulled back together. That's when God's blessing and anointing come on your life.

It doesn't matter what people seem to be getting away with. It's not important that other kids are sneaking around without their parents knowing about it. One day, people will be wondering why you have a car, although you're only sixteen, why your parents allow you to go overseas on mission trips, or why they allow you to do other really cool things. It is simply because God's blessing is on your life. You will have a much happier life with more fulfillment and you can do more things than if you had played the world's game.

Memorize Ephesians 6:1–3 today. Think about what you can do today and this week to honor your mother and father. List four or five things you will do this week to show your parents that you are honoring them.

1. _____

2. _____

3. _____

4. _____

5. _____

WHAT IS HONOR?

Many people are confused about the difference between honoring and obeying. As children, we need to obey our parents. However, as we grow older, we can make a decision to honor our parents. Some people may find it difficult to honor their mom and dad because of some things their parents have done or said that have not been very godly.

Maybe your parents aren't saved. You might be thinking, *How can I honor my mom and dad if they don't even love the Lord?* When you honor others, you respect them because of the position they hold. You don't necessarily honor them because they deserve it or because of anything they have done. You honor them because the position is worthy of honor.

Presidents of countries all over the world travel with grand entourages. Parades are held in their honor, people salute them, crowds cheer them, and other countries roll out the red carpet for them. Wherever they go, they are given great honor. Some of them may be terrible leaders. They may have policies that don't make sense. The way they dress may be really funky. They may be really boring speakers. However, because they are leaders of countries, people give them honor.

It is the same way with your parents. They may do things you don't like. They may have rules in your house that you don't agree with. You may not like their clothes or the way they do their hair. You may not like the food they fix or their hobbies. They may have habits that irritate you. All of that aside, God has given them specific positions as your parents.

Of all the people in the world, He chose those two to bring you into the world. He could have used anybody, but He chose those two. Why? Who knows why? It was God's decision, and He gave them the positions of being your biological parents. They are, by virtue of their positions, worthy of receiving your honor. So, whether or not you like what they do, whether or not you like their rules and regulations, God says that He will bless you if you honor them.

Right now is the time to begin to honor your mom and dad, no matter what they've done or said. It's time to begin to esteem them because of the positions God gave them. Honoring is not based on whether you feel like it; it's a decision you make. You have to say, "I know God gave my parents their positions, and I'm going to make a decision to honor them, no matter how I feel and no matter what they've done. I will honor them because they are my mom and my dad."

CHALLENGE 7: Commit to Honor Your Parents

DAY 3

REBELLION EQUALS WITCHCRAFT

1 Samuel 15:23
For rebellion is as the sin of witchcraft,
And stubbornness is as iniquity and idolatry.

Take five minutes to memorize this Scripture. Write it out in your own words. Write what you think it would sound like in 1990s teenage language.

_____

_____

_____

_____

_____

The Bible says that rebellion is just like the sin of witchcraft. Most of us would agree that we would never want to become involved with witchcraft because we don't want demons in us. Most of us don't want to fool around with the occult. But the Bible says that rebellion is just like the sin of witchcraft. Of course, we know that God looks at all sin equally. Whether you murder someone or you lie to someone, it's all sin. However, rebellion has an added twist to it.

God is very serious about the authorities that He sets up in our lives. He wants us to obey and honor them. He has given your parents authority in your life. He knows that when you buck the authority system that He has set up in your life—when you rip it up and disrespect it—you are disrespecting what God has put in your life to help you develop into a responsible young man or woman for Him. He has put these guidelines and people in your life to protect you. When you go against them, you get out of the protection of God. In other words, you make yourself open game for the devil when you rebel against your parents. When you disrespect them and you dishonor them, you make yourself a target for Satan.

Rebellion seems to be at an all-time high in terms of popularity. Young people brag about how they sneaked around on their parents, what they've gotten away with, or how they got to do things and their parents never found out. It makes you feel as if you have to compete with that if you're going to have any fun. Other people may show rebellion by calling their parents by their first names, using a certain tone of voice with their parents, or manipulating their parents (that is, playing Mom against Dad) to get away with what they really want to do. It may be the typical thing to do, but it's all rebellion. It's all an act of disrespect and dishonor.

When you begin to toy with this command, you get out of God's protection and become an open target for the devil. It's just like witchcraft. You might as well go ahead and do witchcraft because that's how bad it is. God's protection plan is better than "you're in good hands with Allstate." You're in perfect hands with God when you do what He desires for you to do as a young man or woman of God.

As a WorldChanger, you agree you would *never* want to touch witchcraft. You need to have the same kind of conviction and fervency about the way you treat your parents. You would *never* want to be in any kind of rebellion, even slight rebellious attitudes. There are going to be times when your parents ask you to do things you don't want to do. You have to decide if you are going to walk in rebellion or if you are going to walk in submission.

> **"Missions is . . . 'becoming the body of Christ to all the world.'"**
> —Paul

For the rest of your life, you will need to submit to some people. You will need to submit to your boss. The Bible tells husbands and wives to submit to each other. Wherever you live, you will need to submit to the government. It won't always be easy to submit. You have to make a decision: if God has put these authorities in my life, then I am going to comply with the things that they are going to ask of me.

As a WorldChanger, you have to be absolutely committed that you want no part of any kind of rebellion in your life. You will not let the devil have any part of your heart. It doesn't matter if other people seem to be getting away with things. You know that it's total rebellion, and you won't even be jealous of the things they get to do. You would rather look like a submissive stick-in-the-mud than a popular rebellious teen because you know it is pleasing to God to be submissive to your parents.

List some areas here in which you have been rebellious to your parents.

_____

_____

_____

Commit right now to make a drastic turnaround in these areas and to be radically submissive to your parents and pleasing to the Lord.

"Missions is . . . 'spreading the Word of God to a dying world.'"

—Sam

Day 4

An Attitude of Honor

Ephesians 4:23

Be made new in the attitude of your minds (NIV).

Philippians 2:5

Your attitude should be the same as that of Christ Jesus (NIV).

Take some time to memorize Philippians 2:5 right now. Study it until you can say it five times without looking.

When we talk about honoring parents, attitude is a major area that we need to examine. Write down what you think it means to have the same attitude as that of Jesus Christ. What kind of attitude did He have?

_____

_____

_____

_____

_____

Many times you might say, "Well, I'll be obedient to my mom and dad, but I won't be happy about it." You have to ask yourself if you're really honoring them when you obey with a bad attitude. For example, your mom tells you to take out the garbage, but you're watching TV. She says it again and again. Finally, you get up, stomp out of the room, take out the garbage, sigh real heavily and mumble stuff under your breath, and stomp back in—making sure everyone knows that you're really mad. Did you obey your mother? Yes. Did you honor her? No! You obeyed in that instance after being asked several times, but you didn't honor her. It's not enough to just do the thing. You have to do it with an honorable attitude and a submissive, joyful spirit. God will bless you for having the right attitude.

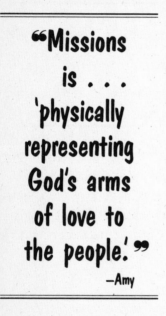

"Missions is . . . 'physically representing God's arms of love to the people.'"

—Amy

Your attitude makes all the difference. It's your choice about the kind of attitude you have. As a World-Changer, you're not manipulated by some circumstance. You don't say, "I don't feel like doing this, so I'm going to get mad and stomp my feet." You're bigger than that. You have the God of the universe living inside you. You want to live for Him with all your heart. You want to change the world and do incredible things in your school and all over the place. You can choose to have the same attitude as that of Christ Jesus: a humble, submissive heart toward your mom and dad, bending over backward to do whatever they want you to do.

The attitudes of the world may have infected you so much that you don't even realize that when you stomp your feet, you're displaying the attitude of the world. Many times you may say things about your parents behind their backs. It's time for you as a World-Changer to stand up and be counted as someone who loves your parents and honors them. You honor them by making them look good in front of other people. You honor them when you don't let them look bad.

When you get around your friends and they start putting down their moms and dads, start lifting up your parents. Your mom and dad aren't perfect; they have done wrong things. Honor them because you want God to bless your life. When others talk about how mean their moms and dads are, you say, "God gave me my parents and I love them. I'm glad they are a part of my life. Sometimes they tell me to do things I don't want to do, but I honor them anyway. I listen to them because they have given me some great advice."

I want to encourage you to have an attitude that would absolutely blow your mom and dad away. Develop an attitude that causes other people (teenagers or adults) to be blown away because they see in the way you treat your mom and dad the same attitude in you as that in Christ Jesus.

Let me give you some specific tips on how to change your attitude. When your mom and dad talk to you, don't say things under your breath. Look them right in the eye and answer them with honor, dignity, and respect. Answer them with a "yes, sir," or "yes, ma'am." It doesn't matter whether you're from the South or not. You need to start honoring your parents when you talk to them. Let it be reflected in your attitude.

> **"Missions is . . . 'spreading God's love to a dying world, an opportunity to give the world what they're looking for.'"**
>
> —Matt

Another specific thing to give attention to is your tone of voice. Don't yell at your parents. You should never, ever raise your voice with your parents. Never, ever say anything out of anger or disrespect. Hold your tongue. Listen to what you're saying and thinking.

Something else to avoid is talking about your parents behind their backs. Don't talk about them when they're not around or when they're in the other room. Don't mutter under your breath as you walk away. Treat them with respect. Never run your parents down. If you have a problem with your mom and dad, talk with them about it. Work out the situation like mature Christians. If you don't feel that you can work it out with your mom and dad, talk to your pastor or youth pastor in a confidential situation. Even if your parents aren't saved, your pastor or youth pastor can help you come up with a workable solution. Don't go running down your mom and dad all around town, making them look bad. Your own mouth will make you look bad in the end. Show this world that you're a Christian with an honorable attitude toward your parents.

Write down some things that you can do today that would change your attitude in areas where you have had a bad attitude. Commit to do these things today.

DAY 5

OBEY WITH YOUR WHOLE HEART

Ephesians 6:5–8

> *Slaves, obey your earthly masters with respect and fear, and with sincerity of heart, just as you would obey Christ. Obey them not only to win their favor when their eye is on you, but like slaves of Christ, doing the will of God from your heart. Serve wholeheartedly, as if you were serving the Lord, not men, because you know that the Lord will reward everyone for whatever good he does, whether he is slave or free* (NIV).

In these verses, the Bible is talking about slaves obeying their earthly masters. Although I know you might feel like a slave to your mom and dad, that's not what I'm trying to imply here. The point is this: God is giving you some principles for how you should respond to authority in your life. Verses 6–7 say, "Obey them not only to win their favor when their eye is on you, but like slaves of Christ, doing the will of God from your heart. Serve wholeheartedly." That's the kind of attitude you want to have toward your parents. Whether they're looking at you or not, you're going by their wishes because that honors them. Maybe they weren't home and never would have caught you when you came in late, but you are going to honor their word and their guidelines by being honest with them.

You want to bend over backward to do whatever you possibly can to honor your parents. Don't just go by the letter of the law; go by the spirit of the law. Don't come in two minutes after curfew and argue about whether or not you were late; come in half an hour early! Go crazy to show them that you're not trying to get away with anything, but you want to have a servant, submissive heart. What you're really doing is pleasing the Lord. God is pleased with a heart that is submissive, not just barely trying to get by with the letter of the law.

You want to do more than what your parents expect from you. If they ask you to wash the dishes, sweep and mop the kitchen floor as well. If they ask you to make your bed, clean your whole room. I know it could take years to get your whole room clean, but next time it should go faster. Show them from your heart that you're not just doing barely enough to get by. Do more than they ask of you. Go overboard because you want to be sure they understand beyond a shadow of a doubt that you are someone who has a submissive attitude toward them and you're honoring them in what you do.

List three or four areas where you could go overboard today to really show your mom and dad that you're not just doing what they say, but you're doing what they wish, what they really want.

1. _____

2. _____

3. _____

4. _____

Your perspective toward your parents should be, "Your wish is my command. I don't want to do just what you tell me, I want to do what you really want me to do. I know in doing that, I'll be pleasing to the Lord." Meditate on Ephesians 6:5–8, and think about what it really means to serve your parents wholeheartedly.

CHALLENGE 7: Commit to Honor Your Parents

DAY 6

HOW TO HONOR

We are talking this week about honoring your parents. I want to talk about some specific ways you can honor your parents.

First of all, you can honor your parents by listening to them. The Bible says, "He who answers a matter before he hears it, it is folly and shame to him" (Prov. 18:13). Most young people don't want to listen to what their parents have to say. They're tapping their feet or sighing loudly or watching TV. Whatever the method, they're not really tuned in and listening to their parents.

It's time to stop everything, chill out, and listen to what Mom and Dad are saying. Maybe they're giving you some advice. Maybe they're telling you something that's really going to protect you and keep you from messing up your life. Maybe it will help you get through college. Maybe it's a tip that will help you in a relationship or a friendship. Even if it sounds boring or it doesn't make sense, the Bible says that if you're going to be respectful, you really need to listen. Just because you're a Christian, someone who loves God, you should be respectful enough to tune in to another person whom God has given authority and responsibility for you. You should be particularly respectful of your mom and dad.

List some things right now that you can do, or stop doing, that would help you really listen when your mom and dad are talking (for example, look them in the eye, turn down the TV, put down your magazine, etc.).

_____

_____

_____

_____

_____

Another thing you can do to really honor your parents is to obey them. I mentioned obedience earlier, but let's deal with it specifically. They will want you to do some things that you don't want to do. To be quite honest, you need to go ahead and do them anyway. If you always wanted to do everything they wanted you to do, then there would never be any challenge to it. The challenge is obeying even when they ask you to do things that are uncomfortable or inconvenient for you to do. We talked yesterday about bending over backward to obey the spirit of the law rather than just the letter of the law.

If your parents are asking you to do some things that are blatantly against Scripture, and you don't know whether you should do them or not, I want to encourage you to talk to your pastor or youth pastor about these things. As they see that these things are against Scripture, let them talk to your parents with you and help you work through this situation.

I want to encourage you to blow your parents away by how quickly you obey. Don't drag your feet. Don't make any negative comments. BOOM! Blow them away because you do more than they ask.

DAY 7

HONOR YOUR PARENTS BY SHOWING RESPONSIBILITY

Probably the best way you can honor your parents is by showing them you are responsible. Show them that you have really learned the stuff they have been teaching you all these years. Let them see you applying it to your life. Show them that your life is more together than it was and beginning to prosper because you really have been listening to what they have been telling you.

Show that you are responsible by driving carefully. Do you have any tickets? Do you run red lights? Do you go faster than you should? Show that you are responsible by getting good grades. Show that you are responsible by spending your allowance or work money wisely. Do you blow it all on pizza, or are you saving some and putting it away? Don't always ask them for a handout, even for valid things like clothes or food. Show them that you are responsible by using some of your own money.

Don't be a couch potato or a slug. How do you spend your spare time? Do you play video games or sit in front of the TV all the time? Or are you doing something to improve yourself and to do something with your life? You could even help out with chores around the house. Show your mom and dad that you can be trusted. When they give you a little area of responsibility, be faithful in that so they can give you more.

A great way to show your parents that you are responsible is to develop an accountability relationship with them as we discussed a few weeks ago. Go to them and say, "I really want to be submissive. I want to be obedient. I really want you to get in my face if you see anything in my life that's not like Jesus. I so desperately want to grow to be like Him. I know that you two are the closest people in my life, and you can see things that I may need to change to be more like Him." Show them this kind of attitude, and they will see a responsible maturity about you. You will be amazed at the freedom they will give you.

As a WorldChanger, you need to make a commitment today. Make a vow that no matter what the rest of the world does, you are going to be someone who listens to your mom and dad, respects and honors them, and submits to them because you know that God's blessing will blow your face off.

"Missions is . . . 'going out and preaching the gospel."

—Joel

I commit all through my teen years to honor my parents, obey them, and listen to them in everything I say and do. I refuse to walk in rebellion or in attitudes that will reflect any dishonor to them. I want everyone to see that the way I treat my parents is the way God wants me to treat them.

_____   _____
WorldChanger's Signature   Date

Week 10

Challenge 8:
Commit to Your Church and Your Youth Group

DAY 1

ATTENDING

Hebrews 10:25

Some people have gotten out of the habit of meeting for worship, but we must not do that. We should keep on encouraging each other, especially since you know that the day of the Lord's coming is getting closer (CEV).

The Bible is specifically talking about the importance of getting together with other Christians so that you can learn and grow and continue going for God with all your heart. A lot of people think that as long as they make their commitment to the Lord, they can do whatever they want as long as they don't fall into major sin.

The point is, as we talked about earlier in the book, you are not designed to be a Lone Ranger Christian. You are designed to do incredible things for God and to change the world, but you have to be connected with other people who want to do the same thing. In this passage, the Bible is giving specific instruction and saying, "Don't you dare quit going to church! Don't you dare stop getting together with people who have like mind and like faith."

This is a big word to young people today. A lot of people say, "I can't really make it to church. My job or my sports interfere with my church and youth group." You have to have people around you. The Bible calls it fellowship. You have to surround yourself with people who love God and are going for God in the same direction.

I have talked to so many youth pastors who get really discouraged. It seems they work their hearts out for their young people, and yet the young people don't seem very committed. For example, the youth pastors will plan and plan and plan some kind of retreat or activity. They put it on the announcement board for two months and mention it during meetings. And when it's time for the activity, no one comes. It turns out that the teenagers are more committed to a school activity or sport than they are to this group of people with whom they are going to heaven and spending eternity.

As a WorldChanger, you need to turn that reputation around. You need to be the kind of person who says, "I know God has plugged me in here. God has a plan and a reason for my being here. I'm going to do everything I can to make sure that I'm here. I'll not commit to just Wednesday nights or just Sunday mornings. But every time that there is an opportunity for me to grow, I'm going to be here." Does that mean you have to be there every time the doors are open to the church? No. But at the very least, be committed to the regular services that your pastor and youth pastor have going so that they know you are a serious Christian.

Don't be an airhead floating around saying, "I have my Bible and my study manual, and I'll do my own thing." You have to be plugged in to a local group of people. If you are committed to the Lord, then there ought to be other people around you who know about your commitment to the Lord and who can help you grow.

Maybe you have done some things that I've mentioned here or even other things to show a lack of commitment to your pastor or youth pastor. I want you to take a moment and think through anything you may have done to express that attitude to your youth group or to your church. Take some time this week to ask your youth pastor and pastor to forgive you for anything you have done to make their jobs more difficult.

Think of some things that you can do that will show your commitment. How can you show that you have determined that you will not allow yourself to get out of the habit of meeting for worship? How can you show your commitment to your youth group and church? Don't just be a flighty, airheaded, haphazard

Christian who floats in now and then. Write down four or five ways that you can show your commitment.

1. _____
2. _____
3. _____
4. _____
5. _____

Take Hebrews 10:25 and memorize it today so that it becomes a part of your life and your heart.

CHALLENGE 8: Commit to Your Church and Your Youth Group

DAY 2
SPUR ONE ANOTHER ON

Hebrews 10:24

And let us consider how we may spur one another on toward love and good deeds (NIV).

If you'll notice, this verse is written right before the verse you memorized yesterday. Take a few minutes and memorize Hebrews 10:24 right now.

I want you to write out in your own words what it means to spur one another on toward love and good deeds.

One reason it's so important to regularly meet together and have real commitment to your church and your youth group is to continue to push each other on to be more like Jesus. It's another area of accountability. We talked earlier about having accountability friendships. You need to have two or three people you are very close with, but that's not enough. You also have to be tied in to a local body; these people know your life, and you know their lives. You need to be in a place where you're being fed and you're growing, and where you're submissive to the leadership that God has put there. As you get into a youth group in a church, you have the opportunity to do exactly what the Scripture says. You can reignite your fire for God, really love each other, and help each other do good deeds.

It's like this: God wants every youth group to be full of World-Changers. He wants every church to be full of people who will change the world. As you get committed, you are saying, "I want to push you to love and good deeds. I want to help you get other new ideas on how we, as an army, can really change this world." You can't be a part of an army if you show up only now and then so that nobody can count on you. If others were counting on you, but you didn't show up or you showed up without your weapon, you just blew the whole war.

As a WorldChanger, you have to decide to get plugged in and

stay plugged in. You have to do everything you can to be a part of this thing. You have to say, "I'm a part of the team. I'm a part of the family. I'm a part of this particular army. I'm going to be a part of what God is doing here. We're going to push each other on toward love and good deeds. I'm not just going to try to push myself and spur myself on, but I'm going to let other people speak into my life and other people spur me on. We are going to be a part of an army and do everything we can to put our heads together to find out how we can really invade and overtake this world with the love of Jesus."

CHALLENGE 8: Commit to Your Church and Your Youth Group

DAY 3

A SENSE OF BELONGING

1 Corinthians 6:20
> *You were bought at a price; therefore glorify God in your body.*

Let's talk about what it means to be bought at a price. The Bible says we have all been bought at a price. Jesus paid His blood for you. If you have given your heart to Him, then you don't belong to yourself anymore because He bought you. He owns you because you have freely given your life to Him. You don't give your life to Him and then live for yourself; you give your life to Him, and then you belong to Him. Think about this.

Too many young people don't really consider that they belong to their youth group. They belong to their sports teams or choirs or bands or some other clubs. But they don't really belong to their youth group. They just go because Mom and Dad go to that church. Their identity is wrapped up in other things they do, such as the cars they drive or the people they hang around.

As a WorldChanger, you need to change the sense of belonging. I assume if you're this far in the book, you really have given your whole life to the Lord. If this is true, then you are in the same group as other people who also belong to the Lord. They have given their lives, so they belong to Him; you have given your life, so you belong to Him. You belong with each other, and with them, you should find the most sense of belonging.

What does that mean? Other WorldChangers, other people who are radically committed to God, are the ones you're talking about when you say, "These are my blood brothers, my blood sisters. These are the people I'm tight with. That's where my heart is, my gut is. All of my plans revolve around them. The most important thing I can do revolves around other World-Changers, people who really want to make a difference, the people in my youth group, the people in my church who are really making a difference in the world."

When you are thinking this way, you don't look at something the church has planned and say, "I can't really do that because I have plans with my sport or my school." You change the whole thing around: "I really belong to the wild group of WorldChangers who want to shake up my community and the world. If there are plans with my WorldChanger group, I really want to participate. They are the ones I really belong to because I'm going to be living with them forever. If they have plans, then I'll cancel anything that interferes because my real identity is not found in football or basketball or cheerleading. My real identity is found in what we are doing for God to change this world. That's what I'm made of; that's what's eating me up on the inside; that's what I'm about! I belong with people who belong to Christ. That's where the true core of what I am lies."

To say that you will cancel anything that interferes is not to say that you will not be a person of your word. As a World-Changer, you have to be a man or woman of integrity. However, you may want to avoid getting involved with groups whose activities regularly conflict with your youth group schedule. Or you could talk with your coach or other leader and tell him or her that you have a commitment to your youth group but want to participate when there's not a conflict. That would be a good way to make a strong statement about your beliefs. You definitely want to make youth group activities a higher priority than anything like parties, dances, or sporting events where you're just a spectator.

Now this is pretty radical thinking. Most young people go to youth group, but they belong somewhere else. Right now is the time for you to rethink why you are in the youth group. If you really love God as you say, then you need to start pouring your energy into the things that your youth group and your church are trying to accomplish.

I want you to make a list of things that you feel you belong to or that you are really tight with right now.

How do you think you can change your sense of belonging so that you're more committed to your youth group and to your church than these other things?

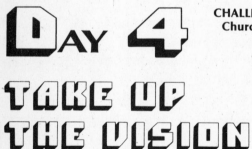

Make some decisions today to get more committed to the vision of your youth group and the vision of your church and to feel more at home there than you do anywhere else because you're with people who belong together as people bought at a price by Jesus.

DAY 4

CHALLENGE 8: Commit to Your Church and Your Youth Group

TAKE UP
THE VISION

Colossians 3:23

Whatever you do, do it heartily, as to the Lord and not to men.

God knows that all people long to find something they can do heartily. They want to find something they can throw their hearts and minds into. I think one of the biggest problems today is that young people are trying to find something to pour their lives and their guts into. They are looking for something they can give their all for, so they get into something that demands everything. Some people pour their lives into academics or a career. Some get involved in sports or other worthwhile activities, but some get caught up in drugs or gang activity. Although these don't seem to have anything in common, they serve as examples of the wide variety of distractions available for teens. They distract from the main thing we were designed to pour our hearts into. We should get our sense of purpose from pouring our all into the things of God and the thing He has called us to do.

We humans are made with the tendency to pour our lives into something. That's why the Bible says, "Love the Lord your God with all your heart, soul, and strength." You ought to pour your life into the things of God. Yes, you can be involved in other interests for fun, but He wants your heart to be into helping promote His kingdom. He knows that when you pour your life into it, you'll be the most fulfilled.

Let me get more specific. God has given you a church and a youth group for a reason. He has given your youth pastor and pastor a vision for what they want to do to shake up and change your city, your town, your area, your region. It is absolutely imperative for you, as a WorldChanger, to become involved with the vision that your youth pastor and pastor have for your church and your youth group to shake up the world. They have to know that your heart is there, your guts are there, your soul is there. You want to do everything you can to blow that thing wide open

> **"Missions is . . . 'laying down my life for the cause of Christ.'"**
>
> —Emily

and to make it awesome and totally successful. You want to show the world that God is doing something through your youth group. It has to have your identity, your sense of belonging.

You need to say, "The most happening thing God is doing in town, next to my quiet time, is what God is doing in my youth group. We're shaking up the city. We're invading the hangouts. We're turning over the junior high. We're turning over the senior high. We're strategically intervening at all the sports games to cause revival at halftime. We're doing stuff that really makes a difference. It's not just that I'm sort of involved, or I come when the youth pastor begs me. I'm there before he wants me there, and I'm praying for it and planning for it. I'm taking notes, and I'm volunteering my time because I'm radically committed with all of my heart to this vision that God has given my youth pastor and my pastor. In fact, I have taken it on as my own. It's not just their vision or the church's vision; it's my vision because I'm a part of this church and this youth group. I'm going to pour my guts into doing everything I can to make this happen."

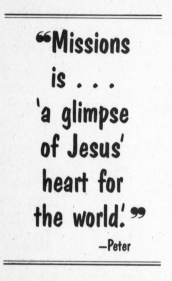

"Missions is . . . 'a glimpse of Jesus' heart for the world.'"

—Peter

You need to take some time to meet with your youth pastor (and maybe your pastor, depending on how big your church is) and ask him where you fit into the vision. Tell him you have some free time, and you want to really pour your life into this thing. Ask him about his vision and how you can help to further that vision. Tell him you want to be more than an attendee. You want to be someone whose heart, soul, and guts are totally sold out to this thing.

Memorize Colossians 3:23 today. Meditate on it and chew on it all day long. List some things here that you can do to further the vision of your church or youth group.

Schedule an appointment with your youth pastor today, and let him know about your commitment to the vision. Get clear directions from him about what you can do to further that vision. Do it with all your heart, and you will have so much fulfillment that you won't know what to do with yourself.

One more thing for you to think about: If you are genuinely committed to the vision, you give and tithe to your youth group and church each week. If you are really pouring your heart into it, your money will naturally follow. And if you give and tithe to your local fellowship, God will bless you for it.

> **"Missions is . . . 'flexibility. Jesus is the Lord of the way I feel.'"**
>
> —Erica

DAY 5

SUBMIT TO YOUR YOUTH PASTOR

Romans 13:1

Everyone must submit himself to the governing authorities, for there is no authority except that which God has established. The authorities that exist have been established by God (NIV).

As a WorldChanger, you have to be committed to the vision of your youth group and your church, and you need to be specifically committed to your youth pastor and loyal to him or her. I mentioned a few days ago that many youth pastors feel all alone. They're doing this thing called youth ministry, and they feel like they have to drag all the young people along with them.

A WorldChanger doesn't have to be dragged. A World-Changer drags other people along to jump into what the youth pastor is already doing. A WorldChanger is not someone who mocks the youth pastor and lets him worship all by himself or preach all by himself while everyone else is drifting off. A WorldChanger bends over backward to be submissive to the youth pastor.

A lot of the same principles I talked about regarding showing submission and respect to your parents apply to your youth pastor. If he asks you to stop talking, you don't start writing notes instead. In fact, you shouldn't have been talking in the first place. You should be bending over backward to show yourself as an example to others of the kind of attitude they should have toward the youth pastor. You don't want to be talking behind his back. You don't want to be running him down into the ground. You don't want to be whispering malicious rumors about him or your dislike of certain things he does. If there is something you dislike about what he has said, then be honest enough to go to him face-to-face. If he changes his mind, fine. If he doesn't, say, "I'm committed to this vision. I'm committed to you. I'm going to shut my mouth and go along with this." It takes a big man or woman to realize and live with disagreements. God has given you this leader, and you need to submit.

Being loyal to your youth pastor is having the attitude that you believe God has placed you in that group and God has placed him or her over you, and that you are going to listen to and follow your youth pastor with a great attitude.

Being respectful to your youth pastor means you're going to honor him and obey him. It means you'll listen to him. You're going to take notes about his preaching. You're going to worship. It doesn't mean that you have to agree with everything. But you will be wholeheartedly committed to his vision. Being respectful and loyal to your youth pastor means that when there is a school activity and a youth group activity at the same time, you choose what he has organized rather than a school activity.

I know that sounds radical and like it's over the edge. But it should be typical behavior. God's activities are more important than any school activity, but a lot of people just go to a youth group because their moms and dads go to that church.

> **"Missions is . . . 'using your life to change someone else's.'"**
> **—Nancy**

A WorldChanger has a different attitude, though. You don't just go there because your mom and dad go to that church. You go to the youth group because God has His plan in this whole thing. God put you there as a part of that group, and God put that leader there in charge of you. By honoring that leader, you are honoring God. God will bless your life, and you will be amazed at how much leadership you will develop by learning to really follow and submit.

You can find many examples in the Scriptures. For example, in Acts 16:3, when Paul wanted to take Timothy along on a journey, Paul circumcised him because the Jews who lived in that area knew Timothy's father was Greek. Timothy submitted to Paul even to the point of being circumcised, even though it was clear that no one was saved by circumcision. Wow! If he could do that, surely you can submit to your youth pastor and pastor. What they want you to do would never be this drastic! The leaders who are over different areas of your life are there because God put them there. Now it's time to wholeheartedly respect and honor them. Respect and honor your youth pastor because he or she has been placed there by God.

List some things that you may have done that have dishonored or been disrespectful of your youth leader.

_____

_____

_____

List some things that you will do this week to show him in an incredible way that you are going to honor him, listen to him, and obey him from this point forward.

Take a few minutes now to memorize Romans 13:1. Make the appointment with your youth pastor this week to ask her to forgive you in any areas where you have dishonored her. Ask her how you can get plugged in to the vision. Tell her of your commitment to the vision.

CHALLENGE 8: Commit to Your Church and Your Youth Group

DAY 6

SUBMIT TO YOUR SENIOR PASTOR

Romans 13:1
> *Everyone must submit himself to the governing authorities, for there is no authority except that which God has established. The authorities that exist have been established by God (NIV).*

A WorldChanger is respectful of the senior pastor and the leadership of the church (the elders and other leaders). It doesn't just all revolve around your youth group. You are also a member of your church at large. If you're really going to be a World-Changer, you need to know how to display the right kind of attitude toward your pastor.

Sometimes young people come in with a cocky attitude, and it's very, very disrespectful to the leaders of the church and to the pastor himself. Too many young people think, *My youth pastor can relate to me, but the pastor of my church is old and can't really relate*. They mock him or pass notes or throw spit wads in the back row. The attitude of a WorldChanger should be completely different from that. God will not permit you to be that way. If you want God to bless your life, you need to honor leadership at every level He gives you. Your pastor is one of the leaders.

You can do some specific things to show your pastor that you respect him. Sit in the front row instead of the back row. Join in the worship service. Look him right in the eye when he looks at you. On the way out, shake his hand and say, "Pastor, I appreciate you. Thank you for speaking into my life."

Take notes through the sermon and really try to get a lot out of his message. If you open up your heart and say, "God, please help me to really listen to what You are speaking to me today," you'll be amazed at what God will speak through your pastor, even though he is older and from a different generation. After all, the Word of God is thousands of years old, and it still relates to you. So what if your pastor is a little bit older than you? He can still relate.

You can also show your pastor that you respect him by the way you dress. A lot of young people come to church dressed like they're going to hang out with their friends. God doesn't care what you look like on the outside, but your appearance can show an attitude of respect or disrespect. Think about it this way: if you were going to meet with the president of the United States or some other country, how would you dress?

Would you dress like a slob and leave your shirttail hanging out and have messy hair?

As I travel to churches around the country, I see many young people dressed like that. It's true that we're going to the house of God to meet with the Lord almighty, and of course, He looks at our hearts. But we should care enough about the way we carry ourselves that we look at least a little respectful. Does that mean you have to wear a shirt, tie, and suit or a dress every time? No. But maybe you should try it at least now and then. Care about how you carry yourself and put yourself together because you communicate to the pastor and the church whether or not they're important to you by how you dress. If you would dress up to meet a government official like a president or a governor, wouldn't it be more important to dress up to meet with somebody who is in leadership in the household of God? With someone who has spiritual authority in your life? With someone who is pouring his life into you way more than any government official? Honor him by how you carry yourself and how you look.

List some things you will do this week to begin to show your pastor and church leaders that you want to honor them and respect them.

Lined writing box for notes

DAY 7

YOUNG AND RADICAL

1 Timothy 4:12

> Don't let anyone make fun of you, just because you are young. Set an example for other followers by what you say and do, as well as by your love, faith, and purity (CEV).

The Bible encourages you not to let anyone mock or look down on you just because you're young. Some people mock teenage Christians and don't take them seriously. They look and dress like slobs, like they're not very committed. They are up and down and back and forth. They're on fire, falling away, on fire, falling away.

As a WorldChanger, you want to change that image. You want to show people that you are part of a force to be reckoned with. You are serious about God, your Christian life, and your commitment to your church and youth group.

Paul tells Timothy to be an example of faith and purity, of love. In other words, young people should be blowing the adults away. The adults should look at the lives of the teens in the youth group and say, "WOW! Why am I not loving people like that? Why don't I have that much respect for my pastor? Why am I not that committed to my church?" Young people should be an example to everyone else. Others should be imitating, not mocking, the youth group.

As a WorldChanger, you need to get a new picture of what your commitment to your church and youth group, to your pastor and youth pastor, is really all about. This is not a haphaz-ard, only-when-it's-convenient thing. Come rain or shine, you're going to church. If the postal carrier can get out in rain, shine, snow, or sleet, why can't you go to church? You say, "Oh, yes, Lord, I'll die for You; I'll do anything for You." But then it gets a little rainy outside and you don't go to church because you might get your hair messy. Hey, that's bogus! You need to have the commitment that says, "Man, I'm going to show myself an example! I don't care if I have to walk the whole way through twenty miles of rain and mud and sleet and hail. I'm going to be there because my heart is there, my guts are there, my commitment is there, my life is there. God has called me to this thing, and I'm pouring my life into it."

Make a commitment today that even though you're young, you'll live the kind of life and have the kind of commitment to your church and youth group that people will look at and say, "Wow! What an incredible example!"

List some things that you can do, or maybe you've already started doing, that will be an example for people to follow.

I commit all through my teen years to my youth group, to my church, to my youth pastor, and to my pastor because I know that it is no accident that I am here. I know that God has given me these leaders and these groups to be involved with to help me grow and to help me change the world. Lord, I commit to find my part in the vision of my church and my youth group and to do everything I can with all my heart to be a part of it.

_____

WorldChanger's Signature   Date

WEEK 11

CHALLENGE 9:
Commit to Start
a Revolution

DAY 1

LOVE WITH ALL
YOUR STRENGTH

Mark 12:30

[Jesus answered him,] "Love the LORD your God with all your heart, with all your soul, with all your mind, and with all your strength."

We've been talking about loving God all through this book, and in this particular week we're going to talk about loving God with all of your strength. That is, using your energy and your strength to really do something for God. What does it mean to love the Lord your God with all your strength? Write out in your own words what you think it means.

Jesus is saying here, "Listen, if you really love God with everything you've got, it ought to affect the way you use your strength!" Think about the way you use your strength or your energy right now. Do you use your energy to expand the kingdom of God? Obviously, in these last few weeks you've been using a lot of energy to grow in the Lord, and that's great. But now it's time to think about how to use your energy as a WorldChanger to really do something to change the world.

People have been talking about changing the world for a long time. They've been thinking about it; they've got plans for it; they've got processes for it and statistics about it. Actually, they've been doing everything but changing the world. It's time for you, as a young maniac who loves God, to start thinking about how you can use your energy to love Him to change this world.

Loving God with all your strength means that while you have strength, while you're alive on this earth, you will make a commitment. You will use the bulk of your energy for God. You will not let your energy get sapped by other interests. You will use your energy to love God! You will find ways to kick the devil in the face and do something about starting a revolution. You will do something that will kick in the doors of hell and let people know that God is alive inside you!

List some ways right now that you've used some of your strength or some of your energy that don't really show that you love the Lord.

Now list some areas that use your energy that don't really show anything. They're neutral; they don't really show that you love the Lord, or they don't really show that you don't love the Lord.

_____

_____

_____

Too many people, maybe even you, use so much of their energy for things that don't give glory to God. They may seem to be doing neutral activities, but they are certainly not working to expand the kingdom of God. God knows that the most exciting, fulfilling life involves pouring your guts and your sweat into loving Him and showing the world that you love Him by what you do.

Think of several things you can do with your energy this week that will show the world your love for Him. Realize that you're not trying to do anything to earn His love because He already loves you so much that He just blows you away with His love. It's the natural response to His love to want to do something out of gratitude for what He's done for you. List two or three things that you could do this week.

1. _____

2. _____

3. _____

Commit today to start doing these things to show the world that you love God.

Day 2

STEP OUT

1 Samuel 14:6

Then Jonathan said to the young man who bore his armor, "Come, let us go over to the garrison of these uncircumcised; it may be that the LORD will work for us. For nothing restrains the LORD from saving by many or by few."

First Samuel 14 shows Jonathan to be a WorldChanger. He was committed to starting a revolution. In this situation, he was involved in a battle where he and six hundred of his men were chased back up into the mountains. They were surrounded by the Philistines, and everything looked bad. The Philistines had kept the Israelites from having anybody to make weapons, so in the whole army, only Saul and Jonathan had any weapons. The men in the army were getting so discouraged that they were beginning to give up hope.

Then in the midst of all these problems, Jonathan got this holy itch. Something began to stir inside him that said, "I can't just sit here and do nothing. I can't sit here and watch the devil run all over us. Who do these people think they are? We are the army of the living God!" Jonathan had this itch and said, "Man, I've got to do something about this!"

Let me ask you today: Do *you* have a holy itch? As you watch the peer pressure at school and you see the devil run all over people's lives, and sometimes the Christians look like so many losers shoved in a corner, does it make you mad enough to want to do something? Do you have a holy itch that says, "I can't stand the way things are, and I've got to do something about it"? Ask God for that holy itch today.

Jonathan did something! He got his armor bearer and said, "Let's go and at least look at these guys and see how big their army is." He said, "Perhaps the Lord will act in our behalf. Nothing can hinder the Lord from saving." Jonathan had this attitude that said, "Just maybe, just perhaps on the slight possibility that God could blow our minds and do something incredible, let's go look at these guys."

"Missions is . . . 'Miracles, Interceding, Servanthood, Sacrifice, Insight, Obedience, No fear, Salvation.'"

Do you have such faith and conviction? It's time for young people to stand up tall and say, "In Jesus' name, I have faith and I have conviction that God is on my side. Just perhaps God will use me to set my campus on fire. Perhaps God will use me and revival will break out during halftime at a ball game. Maybe God will use me and revival will break out in my cafeteria when I stand up to share Christ. Just perhaps God will use me to cause my youth group to explode. Perhaps God will use me to invade another country and get people saved all around the world. Just maybe in the midst of a war that looks like the devil is winning, just maybe God will use me." You need to have the heart and soul of a WorldChanger inside of you.

Your first amendment freedom of speech gives you the ability to do these kinds of things in public places and at school. Just make sure whatever you do is tactful and will be a *positive* witness for Jesus!

I want you to think about 1 Samuel 14 and memorize verse 6 today. Meditate on it and chew on it as you walk through your hallways all day. Meditate on how God will use you. Pray like crazy for God to give you the holy itch that makes you totally uncomfortable watching people around you who are going to hell, that makes you *have* to do something about it!

CHALLENGE 9: Commit to Start a Revolution

DAY 3

GAIN A REPUTATION

Acts 17:6

These who have turned the world upside down have come here too.

Paul and his band of followers had this reputation as they traveled from town to town. As they were brought to court before the officials, this accusation was made against them. Everyone knew their reputation. Everywhere they went, they turned things upside down. They ruffled feathers and stirred things up. They refused to go unnoticed. They never left anything the way it had been before they arrived. Paul had this thing inside him that said, "I cannot stand by and let the devil run this world and mess up people's lives. I don't care what it costs me, I don't care what people say about me or do to me. I have to do something about the evil in this world."

Think for a moment about what people would say about you if they were put on a witness stand and had to account for the kind of Christian you are. Think about your Christian friends. Think about your non-Christian friends. If they had to answer honestly, what kind of reputation would you have? What would they say about the way you live your Christian life? Write out a few sentences telling what they might say about you.

As you are making a commitment to be a WorldChanger, now is your chance to change your reputation. Now is your chance to be the kind of Christian that you always wanted to be. Now is the time to get out of your comfort zone. To make a difference, to change the world, you're going to have to ruffle some feathers. It's time to take a stand and be counted. It's time not just to shake things up for the sake of shaking them up but to shake them up so people's lives can be changed. Bring people to the realization that they can enter into an incredible relationship with Jesus. It's deciding that you're sick of the status quo and you're determined to do something about it. You've been intimidated by the devil and people's opinions way too long.

We have all seen a watered-down Christianity that says all you have to do is go to church, pay tithes, and die to go to heaven and everything will be okay. But that's not the way it is everywhere.

You can join those who have realized it is time to stand up and say, "Man, I'm going to make my life count. I'm going to do something to change this world." List some things that you can do right now to turn things upside down at your school and work and in the lives of people you hang out with.

This is your chance to draw a picture of how you want people to see you. If in six months or a year, you could have any kind of reputation that you could imagine in terms of doing something for God, if you could dictate what people say about you and how you live your life for God, what would you like people to say about you?

Now is your chance to make a decision to do something to change your actions so that they will line up with what you really want people to see in you. You can become the kind of Christian who is making a difference in a very real way. Decide today what you'll do to make this difference and to gain the reputation that you really want to have.

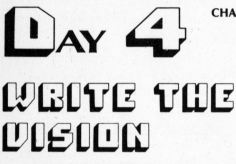

CHALLENGE 9: Commit to Start a Revolution

DAY 4

WRITE THE VISION

Habakkuk 2:2
Then the LORD answered me and said:

> *"Write the vision*
> *And make it plain on tablets,*
> *That he may run who reads it."*

Take a few minutes right now to memorize this verse.

Now that you're stirred up and you've got that holy itch, you're determined to turn the world upside down wherever you go, it's time to really crystallize your vision. Ask God, "What do You want to do through me and with me? How do You want to use me now in my teenage years in my school and in my community? What do You want to do with me through my job, sports, clubs, and youth group? What's Your vision for me, Lord?"

Most young people go from day to day, week to week, and year to year never really thinking, *How does God want to use me right now while I'm young?* God will begin to speak to you as you continue to cram the Word down your throat. As you continue having your quiet times, praying like crazy, and committing to live a holy life, God promises He will speak to you. He says, "My sheep know My voice" (John 10:4, my paraphrase).

He'll speak to you and give you a vision. It's important for you to write the vision down as it says in Habakkuk 2:2. Don't just say, "Well, I think I'll live for God today and do something neat." You have to write it down. You have to make it plain: What do I want to do for God my freshman year, my sophomore year, my junior year, and my senior year? What do I want to do with my summers? Maybe I could go on missions trips, go to the inner city, or really minister and change people's lives here in my own community. What do I want to do in my sports life and my friends' lives and my social life?

You've already talked to your youth pastor about the vision of the youth group. Now you want to find out answers to this: "Okay. God, what part of that vision belongs to me? What do You want me to do?" Part of your vision should definitely be a part of what God is doing through your youth group.

You shouldn't be stumbling through your teen years and your Christian life thinking, *One day I'll grow up, and then I'll really get my vision.* Right now, your vision should be what gives you zest in life, what you lose sleep over, what you can't wait to get up for the next day. What does God want to do in your life, and how does He want to use you to change the world?

You need to stop right now. Slow down and ask, "God, what is Your vision for me? What is Your vision for my sophomore year, my senior year, my freshman year in college? If You could do everything possible through me, what would my school look like in six months? What would my youth group look like in six months if You could do everything You wanted through me? What would my ball team look like in six months or a year? God, if You really could use me and do anything, what would it look like?"

Now I want you to begin to dream. Just imagine and write out your thoughts here. What would your job look like, your ball team, all the different facets of your life? What would your teachers look like? How many of them would have gotten saved? How many of your counselors, advisors, or school administrators would have gotten saved? Dare to imagine and to dream big, and then write that vision down so you have something specific to aim for.

Day 5

COMPELLED TO SPEAK

---

1 Corinthians 9:16

For if I preach the gospel, I have nothing to boast of, for necessity is laid upon me; yes, woe is me if I do not preach the gospel!

Paul is trying to describe what is going on inside his heart and soul. He says, "This thing that is burning inside is so real and so alive, I have to speak it. I have to preach it. I have to get what's inside me out so others can hear it." As a WorldChanger, you should have a life and a relationship with Jesus so real and so alive that there's something burning inside you, something that has to come out.

What you have inside you is an encounter with the living God! This is an encounter with the God who forgave you and gave you a new heart, a new mind, and a new life. This is an encounter with the God who made the whole earth. He has totally, radically, and forever changed you on the inside. This thing has put a new heart in you and a new spirit in you. This thing has given you real life for the very first time! And Paul is saying, "This thing is so real inside me, it's so alive, I've got to get it out. I don't care what people say. I don't care what people do. I've got to start a revolution." And that's exactly what he did. As he went from town to town, he started a revolution and a fire, and he stirred people up.

As a WorldChanger, you've got to journey through life with

the same conviction. You're not just another cheeseball Christian sitting in a pew. You're not just another young person in a youth group somewhere. You've got this thing burning inside you! It's an encounter with God. You can barely describe it in human words, but it's a miracle that has happened inside you. I want to encourage you to begin your day with the same kind of attitude that Paul had. Take five minutes to meditate on 1 Corinthians 9:16. Memorize it, and chew on it. Take it with you all day long. Let this be your motto for today and for this week: "This thing is so real to me, I've got to do something. If I don't say something, this thing will eat me alive!" I want you to take a few minutes to write out some things that you can do today that will really express what you've got inside. Write out what you can say to and do with the people you know you are going to see today to help them understand what you've got living and beating inside your heart.

Now launch forth with boldness and courage as Paul did. Commit to do everything you can. Live life with the conviction that says, "If I don't get some of what's inside me into someone else, I don't know that I'll be able to make it through the day." If you believe and act on that with all your heart, you'll have a great day today, and you *will* change the world.

DAY 6

AVERAGE CHRISTIANITY

Luke 9:1–5

Then He called His twelve disciples together and gave them power and authority over all demons, and to cure diseases. He sent them to preach the kingdom of God and to heal the sick. And He said to them, "Take nothing for the journey, neither staffs nor bag nor bread nor money; and do not have two tunics apiece. Whatever house you enter, stay there, and from there depart. And whoever will not receive you, when you go out of that city, shake off the very dust from your feet as a testimony against them."

Luke 10:1–3

After these things the Lord appointed seventy others also, and sent them two by two before His face into every city and place where He Himself was about to go. Then He said to them, "The harvest truly is great, but the laborers are few; therefore pray the Lord of the harvest to send out laborers into His harvest. Go your way; behold, I send you out as lambs among wolves."

Matthew 28:19

Go therefore and make disciples of all the nations, baptizing them in the name of the Father and of the Son and of the Holy Spirit.

As a WorldChanger, you need to see yourself as a revolutionary. Once in a while, you'll see people witnessing and sharing their faith with other people, but they're the exception to the rule. Too many Christians aren't like that. You, as a WorldChanger, need to change what average Christians look like.

True Christians, according to Jesus' definition, are people who are moving and shaking and stirring things up. Jesus' disciples were examples of this lifestyle. One time He sent them off to villages and towns to cast out demons, heal the sick, and share the gospel of the kingdom of God. Then He brought them back to talk about it before sending them off again with about sixty others to preach, minister, and share. He was so radical, He told them not to take anything with them: "Don't take anything to eat or drink. Don't even pack your bags. Let God supply everything!" Then He said, "Now go and make disciples of the whole world."

> **"Missions is . . . 'real fun.'"**
> —Carolyn

You see, this lifestyle of a WorldChanger, this lifestyle of being a revolutionary and turning things upside down, is not optional. It's not like some people who are really on fire should do this and all the rest should sit in the back pew.

God intends for everyone who joins His army to be involved in a fiery, passionate, committed way to make a difference in the world. It's not just the preachers like Billy Graham who can make a difference. All of us get to make a difference. The thing that makes a difference inside is not just saying, "Okay, I'm going to go make a difference." It's the fact that something has really changed your life. The lifestyle that God wants you to take on is somehow transmitting what He has done inside you into another person. Jesus sent the disciples out once. Then He sent them out again. Ultimately, He sent them out and told them not to come back. In other words, this is the kind of life God wants you to lead. This is the kind of life He wants you to live. This is what your habit should be. This is what you should be doing. This should not be uncommon! This should be what everyone is doing because this is what Jesus commanded all His disciples to do.

I want you to write Luke 9:1–5 out on an index card and take it with you today. I want you to see what the lifestyle of a true disciple of Jesus should be. I want you to chew on it and think about it all day long. Begin to imagine yourself having that as a lifestyle.

You're a revolutionary. You're a WorldChanger. You're going to live on the edge just like those guys did. If you have to take nothing with you, you'll do it. Refuse to fit into the mold of a boring Christian. Step out on the edge and live a lifestyle of doing something to affect this world for Jesus.

CHALLENGE 9: Commit to Start a Revolution

DAY 7

TRANSFER THE POWER

As you think about living the lifestyle of a revolutionary, the life-style of a WorldChanger, one huge question comes to mind. First, I want you to think, *I know God has changed my life. I remember the day I gave my life and my heart to Him. I know the areas of my life He has cleaned up. I know how much He has spoken to me. I know that as He has spoken to me, my life has been changed.*

As you've worked your way through this book, maybe you've been aware that God is dealing with you in different areas of your life, things you've given up and freedom from bondage you were in. That's great! That's incredible! That's exactly what I've been praying for you!

Now the question that comes to mind is this: *How do I get what happened in me, in my relationship with God, to happen in somebody else?* This is the question of the ages. How do we help others to really get connected to God in a way that they fall on their knees and radically convert their lives over to God? This is my life's dream. This is what beats in my heart. This is what I think about all the time. As I'm sitting next to someone on a plane, as I'm preaching to a crowd of people in a developing country, or as I'm preaching to thousands of people every weekend at Acquire The Fire conventions, I ask myself this question: How do I get kids, teenagers, people from another nation, or people who live in a village somewhere to get really connected with God so that God totally blows their minds and changes their lives the way He did mine?

> **"Missions is . . . 'I-lay-me-down sacrifice.'"**
>
> —Jennifer

I believe this is the question of the ages for every person who really wants to change the world. We don't want to get people chanting a meaningless prayer. It's easy to get people to raise their hands and pray, "Lord Jesus, come into my heart." But too many who have done that seem to live the same way they did before. An evangelist can come into town. The leaders can play the music just right, have the choir singing and people coming forward. The lighting can be just right. People can cry and pray a prayer. But none of it is any good if they don't get connected with God.

After you've ministered to somebody and you leave, is he still connected with God? Has she had that heart-to-heart, face-to-face, blow-your-mind, never-the-same experience with God? Sometimes I ask, "God, how did You do it inside me? I was a total heathen. I didn't want You. I was messed up on drugs. My life was being flushed down the toilet. How did You get through to me? Why was it so real to me? What can I possibly say or do to help someone else understand it?"

So many times when we begin to tell people about the Lord, we get into a rut. We mumble, "Well, you know, I . . ." We get the Four Spiritual Laws tract . . . "All have sinned and fall short of the glory of God. And you know, the wages of sin is death . . ." These are true and these are real, but how do I really get the miracle that happened inside me to happen inside them?

I don't know. I think people can mentally say, "Yes, I give my life to Jesus," and still live the same way they lived before and never really get anything done. I believe that WorldChangers, people who want to stir things up, ruffle feathers, and cause a revolution, have to be creative about how they get the gospel to other people.

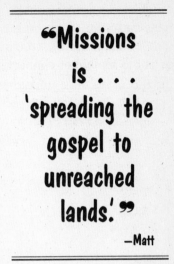

"Missions is . . . 'spreading the gospel to unreached lands.'"
—Matt

You have to be creative about how you communicate, what you say and what you do. Every day, as you are reading the Bible and seeking God, He'll share stuff with you. Keep that stuff, just like a bunch of daggers in your coat pocket, so you've got something to—boom! boom! boom!—hit people with things that just blow their minds. "Wow, where'd you hear that?" they ask. "I heard from God!" you answer.

God will share that kind of stuff with you. But you have to be creative. I want you to take a few moments and write out some creative ways that you can start a revolution in your school. Write out some creative ways that you can communicate the gospel. If you were going to communicate the gospel to someone who worked at McDonald's, how would you communicate it to him? If you were going to communicate the gospel to someone on your football team, how would you say it in a creative way? How would you creatively share the gospel with someone in your chemistry class? I'm not advocating breaking laws or school rules, but there is still a lot you can do for good without violating the rules. Remember, the most important thing here is not a little cheeseball message. It is somehow getting into words the miracle that has happened in your heart so others can glimpse it. Take some time now and write down a creative scenario for each of these three areas.

McDonald's _____

_____

_____

_____

Football _____

_____

_____

_____

Chemistry _____

_____

_____

_____

Now commit today to go and communicate the gospel in a creative way, trying to put into words what has happened to you.

As a WorldChanger, I commit to start a revolution, not to live a boring lifestyle. I commit to do something to get the gospel out right where I live. I will turn this city and this town upside down. I commit to have a reputation like Paul had. I refuse to sit down and watch people go to hell as I just live my life. I have to do something to make a difference, and I have to do something today.

_____   _____
WorldChanger's Signature   Date

WEEK 12

CHALLENGE 10:

Commit to Go on a Mission Trip While You're a Teen

CHALLENGE 10: Commit to Go on a Mission Trip While You're a Teen

DAY 1

PRAY

Luke 10:2

> Then He said them, "The harvest truly is great, but the laborers are few; therefore pray the Lord of the harvest to send out laborers into His harvest."

As a WorldChanger, you want to really change the world. You don't just want to change your community. You're not just committed to ministering to people and stirring up a revolution in your state, region, or country. You want to do something that actually changes the world.

Jesus told His disciples to pray. He didn't give a casual suggestion: "Please pray if you get around to it." He said, "Pray! I mean pray your faces off! I mean let it get under your skin. Feel the heartbeat of God as He cares for the people around the world. Pray that God will raise up laborers, people who will go. Start having a little compassion in your heart about the things that God has compassion in His heart about and pray that God will send people."

Sometimes when you get the idea that you should pray for the people of the world, you pray a little prayer like, "God, please bless those missionaries in China. In Jesus' name, amen." Oh, boy, did God move in that prayer or what? God wants you to really begin to care about the people of the world. He wants you to care enough to do something. The first step is to pray. I mean really pray. Take a book like *Operation World* by Patrick Johnstone and read about different countries. Pray for the unreached people groups in each country. Pray for the people who have never, ever had a chance to hear the gospel even if they wanted to. There is no way for them to hear about Jesus because there is no one to tell them about this Lord in whom we say we believe.

As you and thousands of other young people pledge a commitment to become WorldChangers, your first point of contact to change other parts of the world besides your own neighborhood is to pray. Pray for remote areas. Pray for the missionaries your church supports. Find out everything you can learn about your missionaries and their countries, and pray your face off for them. Look in the encyclopedia, if nothing else, and pray for countries and people who have never had a chance to hear about Jesus. Pray until you feel God's broken heart for them. Pray until you weep and you feel the compassion of God rising up in your heart. Pray that God will raise up people to do something about the tragedy that is happening to millions of people all over the world who have never had a chance to hear about Jesus.

This should be a part of your regular quiet time. Don't just pray about yourself. Don't just stay in the Word and pray for your immediate situation that day. Instead, begin to pray for people around the world on a regular basis so your heart is not just here in America but is around the world. You will begin to get a glimpse of the world the way God sees it. There are pockets of people who have never had a chance to hear the gospel, and God cares about those people. He said He is not coming back until they all get a chance.

Matthew 24:14
And this gospel of the kingdom will be preached in all the world as a witness to all the nations, and then the end will come.

So the first step today is to become involved in praying for people around the world who never have had a chance to hear the gospel. Take some time right now and pray for an unreached people group in a different country from your own.

DAY 2

GO!

Luke 10:3

Go! I am sending you out like lambs among wolves (NIV).

Isn't it interesting that in one sentence Jesus told the disciples to pray with all their hearts for people to go, and then in the next sentence He told the very same people to go? Basically, He told them that they needed to start being the answer to their own prayer. He didn't want them just to sit there and do nothing. He wanted them to go and do something.

Don't be a part of that group of people who just pray and talk about things. Go put some legs on your prayer, and do something about it. He said, "Go!" with an exclamation point. It was not a casual suggestion. It was a thundering "GO!"

Jesus was trying to help the disciples understand that it needed to be a lifestyle. This is not just an opportunity for God to change you. It is an opportunity for you to stir yourself up to go and do something different from the average person who believes.

Go indicates a change of location. It implies movement. Jesus said, "I am sending you out like lambs among wolves." He said, "I know that you are lambs. You are not even sheep yet. You're young. You're not very old and not very strong yet, but I want you to go."

Some young people think, *How can I go? I am just a teenager. How can God use me?* This is the very point that Jesus addresses here. He says, "You're young. You may not have much knowledge of the Bible. You're wet behind the ears—maybe you feel as if you don't have much between your ears—but go anyway."

Maybe you don't feel like a very strong Christian. Maybe you don't feel that there is much substance to your Christian life. You feel that you haven't memorized very many Scriptures. (But you have memorized all the Scriptures in this book so far!) Maybe you don't feel like the best preacher in the world. Maybe you don't even know if you are going to be a missionary for the rest of your life. That is okay. Jesus sent those guys out a couple of times, and many of them came back to Jerusalem and lived there. He said, "I want you to go at least one time because once you have gone, you'll never be the same. Even though you are young, I want you to go."

You may be going through this devotional and you're only thirteen or fourteen years old. That's great! Jesus said, "You might be a lamb, you might be young, but go anyway." He didn't say, "I'm going to use you, even though you are young." I think the point was, *because you are young,* you are still flexible enough, willing to live on the edge enough, to really be used to do something that will change the world.

It is time to blow the excuses out of your head. You are never too young to go. My wife and I have been taking our daughters overseas since they were one and two years old. They go every year, and they look forward to it. God uses the trip to change their lives. Don't let your age keep you back from doing something great and changing the world while you're young.

Begin to pray right now.

God, You said here in Your Word, Jesus told them to go even though they were young, even though they were lambs. God, where do You want me to go? What do You want me to do? What country should I go to? To which people could You use me to bring the gospel?

> **Mark 16:15**
>
> He said to them, "Go into all the world and preach the gospel to every creature."

Memorize this verse, and begin to pray that prayer every day and listen to God as He speaks to your heart.

CHALLENGE 10: Commit to Go on a Mission Trip While You're a Teen

DAY 3

A YOUNG WORLDCHANGER

> **Acts 12:12**
>
> So, when he had considered this, he came to the house of Mary, the mother of John whose surname was Mark, where many were gathered together praying.

I want to show you an incredible example from Scripture of a WorldChanger, a young man named John Mark. You can read in Acts 12 the story of Peter's escape from prison through the miraculous work of an angel. When he realized that he was actually out and that it wasn't a dream, he knocked on the door of a house where a bunch of believers were meeting. He went to the house of Mary, the mother of John also called Mark, where people had gathered and were praying. After some confusion, they let him in the house and realized that it was a miracle. One person in the house was a young man named John Mark. He was maybe thirteen or fourteen years old. He got to hear firsthand how Peter was busted out of jail by an angel. Now read what it says just a few verses later.

Acts 12:25

And Barnabas and Saul returned from Jerusalem when they had fulfilled their ministry, and they also took with them John whose surname was Mark.

So John Mark saw this miracle of Peter being busted out of jail, and before he knew it, he went on a mission trip with Paul and Barnabas. He is an incredible example of a young man who went as a teenager to hang out with Paul and Barnabas on their adventures. He watched them preach the gospel, get thrown in jail, preach the gospel, and get whipped.

John Mark helped Paul and Barnabas start churches all over the place. That is exactly what you would be doing on a mission trip. Acts 13:5:

When they arrived in Salamis, they preached the word of God in the synagogues of the Jews. They also had John as their assistant.

There he was helping them, standing with them, ministering with them, assisting them in any way he could. It is time to do something while you're young just like this young champion John Mark did. This young John Mark is the same Mark who eventually wrote the gospel of Mark. He wrote the whole book from his perspective as a WorldChanger. He started while he was young changing the world and doing incredible things.

What would have happened if his mom or dad had said, "No, you're too young to go on that mission trip"? Maybe the book of Mark would never have been written. What would have happened if John Mark had said, "Well, that was really a neat miracle with Peter, but I don't know about going with Paul and Barnabas. That seems too scary. Man, I heard that they have been in jail. I heard that they get rocks thrown at them when they preach"? John Mark would not let anything intimidate him. You, as a young World-Changer today, cannot let anything intimidate you. Just imagine the incredible things that you could do. God wants to start doing it through you right now while you're young.

I want you to keep praying:

God, where do You want me to go? God, what do You want me to do, even this summer? God, could You use me for a week or a couple of weeks in another country? Could You use me a month or two months somewhere while I am young? God, use me like You used John Mark to change the world while I am young. Help me set a healthy pattern of a lifestyle of a WorldChanger for me to keep for the rest of my life.

CHALLENGE 10: Commit to Go on a Mission Trip While You're a Teen

DAY 4

IT WILL CHANGE YOUR LIFE

Matthew 28:19
Go therefore and make disciples of all the nations, baptizing them in the name of the Father and of the Son and of the Holy Spirit.

Take four minutes and memorize this Scripture. Copy it down and carry it with you all day long.

This is God's mandate for you as a WorldChanger. He calls

you to do whatever you have to do to make your life count for reaching the world. He has not called just a few people to go. This commission is for anybody who calls on the name of Christ.

If you are part of the army of Christ, then you have to be involved in the battle. The battle is on the front lines helping people to hear the gospel who have never heard it before. Your job is to push back the enemy territory. This is not an option. It is not just a good idea for only a few people to take up and do something about. This is for everybody. I believe with all my heart that every single person should go at least one time to take the gospel to another country.

You should go while you're young. You know, some people say that not everybody is called to be a missionary full time. But everybody is called to be involved in reaching the world. When you go *one time,* it absolutely changes your life. You get personally involved in this Great Commission. The Great Commission is not just for a few, but for all people who call themselves Christians.

Once you go and look in the eyes of the people who have never had a chance to hear the gospel and you realize you are the one bringing it to them, it absolutely changes you forever. It spoils you. It messes up your head because you realize that you have a purpose for living here in this world. You will never forget those eyes. Every time your church takes a missionary offering for the rest of your life, you will remember those eyes. You remember the children. You remember the older people. You remember the people who gave their lives to the Lord and are going to heaven because you decided to go on a mission trip. When you wrap your arms around them, you remember their hugging you back. You remember giving them the love of God when you gave your life for a week or a month to bring them the gospel.

As a WorldChanger, you realize that this is part of your life. This is how you are made. You cannot stay at home and forget those people are there. You cannot look at the globe and see it as a ball with pieces of land on it.

People are all around the world. You take God's commission seriously to go. You take it personally. It is not that He is talking to everybody else. He is talking to you. It is as if Jesus is looking you right in the eyes and saying, "You go." Don't assume that somebody else is going to do it. You go. Even if you go only one time, you'll never be the same again.

Continue to pray,

God, where do You want me to go? I am going to take Your commission seriously and personalize it and do something about it. I refuse to let everybody else do the work. I am going to personally do something about it sometime during my teen years. Lord, where could I go this summer?

Let Him begin to speak to your heart about it.

CHALLENGE 10: Commit to Go on a Mission Trip While You're a Teen

DAY 5

DON'T WORRY ABOUT THE MONEY

Probably one of the biggest excuses or objections I hear about going to the mission field is that people don't think they can get the money. Parents are afraid that their teenagers are going to beg money from them, and they don't think they have the money to send their teens. Teens are afraid that their parents will not give them any money and that no one else will either.

Philippians 4:19

And my God shall supply all your need according to His riches in glory by Christ Jesus.

You memorized this verse a few weeks ago in this study. If you haven't already, I want you to copy it down on an index card. Memorize it and meditate on it all day long. Chew on it until it becomes alive for you. You have to realize that God will supply all your needs. He will give you the money that you need to go.

There is no good excuse for not going. The money is an easy thing for God to get. He has tons of money. The Bible says that He owns the cattle on a thousand hills. He will supply your needs. You just have to go and find whose pockets He's keeping the money in. You will have to do some fund-raisers and maybe some car washes. You will need to write some support letters. If you use all the energy you can muster, I guarantee you will get the money.

Getting the money is not the hard part for God. The hard part for God is getting you to say yes. It should be easy because this is such a fun deal. "You mean I get to go to another country? I get a chance to make history? I can help people who have never had a chance go to heaven and people are wanting to say no?" There is no good excuse to say no.

We at Teen Mania Ministries have hundreds of testimonies from teenagers who have raised their money in a week or a month. We have heard phenomenal stories in which God connected the money source and the need just at the right moment. If God has done that for other young people, He will surely do it for you. You have to understand that God definitely wants you to go. And if He wants you to go, then He will help you get the money.

When you apply to go on a Teen Mania mission trip, we send you a whole package of information telling you how to go on a mission trip, what to do, and how to raise money. We put together a whole booklet specifically designed to help you create momentum and excitement about your trip so you can raise money for it. We give you about a million proven ideas. These ideas are taken from other maniacs who have gone before and used these ideas to raise money. Don't dare let money become a hindrance in your stepping out to do something to change the world.

Look at Philippians 4:19, meditate on it all day, and become convinced that God will supply your needs. I know He will, and I know there is a huge world to be reached. God knows that it will take money and people to reach the world, so He will give you the money to go if you will say yes. Keep asking God where He wants you to go. Begin to do something active toward getting on the mission field.

If your youth group has its own mission trip, that is great! Go for it! Get on board and have a blast. If they don't, we would love for you to be a part of a Teen Mania mission trip. I don't care where, but whatever you do *GO!*

CHALLENGE 10: Commit to Go on a Mission Trip While You're a Teen

DAY 6

GOD STILL SENDS PEOPLE

John 3:16
> For God so loved the world that He gave His only begotten Son, that whoever believes in Him should not perish but have everlasting life.

This is a Scripture that you have probably heard ever since you were a kid, but I want you to see something very clearly. The Bible says that God loved the world. It doesn't say that God loved *America* so much that He gave His only Son. The Bible doesn't say that God loved my town or my youth group so that He gave His only Son. It doesn't even say that God just loved me so much that He gave His only Son. The Bible says that He loved the world.

> **"Missions is . . . 'boot camp for God.'"**
> —Peter

When God decided to give His Son, He was looking at all the people all over the world for all time, and His heart was broken. He said, "Man, whatever I have to do to win all the world back, I want to do it." The fact is that more than a billion people still don't know that God sent His Son for the world. They don't know that He loved the world so much that He gave His very best, His Son.

The Bible says that He gave His only Son. He didn't rain tracts down from the sky. He didn't send a fax or an E-mail message. He sent a person. He sent His own flesh and blood because He wanted the people of the world to know that His love was not something abstract. He wanted a human being to come down and show this world what His love was like. He didn't want to just tell people through some written message; He wanted to show them.

So when Jesus came and hugged the children, it was like the arms of God were wrapped around their necks. When He came and gave back dignity to people who were depressed and messed up, they could look in His eyes and see His compassion. When He healed them and placed His hands on them and showed them the Father's love, they could understand and relate to it. They could understand that God loved them so much He sent a human being, His own Son, to show them what He Himself was like.

When God expressed His love to the world, He sent a person, and He still sends people today. He sends people like you and me. He sends people full of the love of God, people who have had a life-changing encounter with God, people full of the fire of a God who gave His life for them. That's the kind of people He sends out to change the world. If you have made a commitment to be a WorldChanger, then you are that kind of person. I believe that you have had an encounter with God and that you will never be the same.

For God so loved the world that He gave His Son. He gave His very best. Let me ask you something: Do you love God so much that you're willing to give your best, to give a summer of your life, to give a month or two months, to give your whole life if necessary? God gave His very best to get the job done, and He is looking for WorldChangers who will give their best to get the job done. He is looking for people who would be willing to complete the job of reaching the entire world.

There is no more time for talk. It is time to get out there and reach the world. As a WorldChanger, you need to stand up and be counted and do something about changing the world.

Pray this prayer:

God, where do You want me to go? I'm ready to go. I'm going to be one of those people who go just like You sent Your Son. I'm ready to go, too, Lord. Send me, and I will go.

If you never have before, memorize John 3:16 right now. Meditate on it today, and really think about the depth of God's love for the world.

DAY 7

IT'S TIME TO GO!

We've been talking about changing the world. We've been thinking about changing the world. You've been getting your heart stirred up about living for God and loving Him and serving Him every day. Now it's time to do something about it. It's time to make plans to go.

We Christians have been talking about changing the world, praying about changing the world, writing books about changing the world, and having conferences about changing the world. But only a few have done much about reaching the world compared to the number of people who claim to be Christians. Most Christians have been doing everything except changing the world! Now is the time to slam on the brakes, stop everything in your life, and say, "Lord, if I don't do anything else, I'm going to make my life count for changing the world. I'm going to do something about it right now."

Whatever plans you have for this upcoming summer, they're *worth changing*. God has a more important agenda. He wants to use you to change the world. Quit leaving it as everybody else's responsibility. It's time to take personal responsibility. As a World-Changer, you are a different breed of Christian. You're someone set apart from the average, boring, lifeless, cheesy, lazy, low-life, couch potato, slug of a Christian. You are somebody who is determined to do something that really matters with your life.

The very fact that you have made it to the end of this book shows that you are determined to go after God with all your heart. Now is the time to step out of your comfort zone and do something about it. You have been praying all along, "Lord, will You use me?

God, do You want to use me?" Now it's time for you to hear His heart say, "Yes, I want to use you. Now go for it!"

Some people are waiting for lightning from heaven or for an audible voice saying, "Go ye, therefore." Well, guess what! He has already said to go. Now it's time for you to obey. He may speak to you in a still, small voice and put a strong desire in your heart. Good! Go for it. The Bible says that He gives you the desires of your heart. He puts the desire inside you to do these things.

Do you feel unspiritual because you just want to go for the adventure? That's okay. It's a valid reason to go, too. What a great adventure to do something for God that will change the world! To be honest with you, that's the first reason I went. I thought it would be fun to reach people for Jesus who have never had a chance to be reached before. As a result, I got a calling to be involved in missions for the rest of my life. God will take a misguided desire to have an adventure or to do just something good for Him and turn it into a life calling.

Make plans right now. Look at the application in the back of this book. Fill it out and mail it to us at Teen Mania. We'll send you all the other information you need. We'll send you details on all the options for the different countries we are going to and how you can get there. You'll be amazed at what God will do through you as you do something about changing the world right now.

Don't be a WorldChanger in name only. Be a WorldChanger in deed. Join the thousands of young people making the commitment to be a WorldChanger. Part of that commitment is doing something to reach out personally to change this world.

God bless you as you make plans to go on a mission trip this summer, as you fill out your application, and as you get ready to raise your money. God is so proud of you that you have made it all the way to the end of this book. You are just at the very beginning of a lifestyle of changing the world. Let your overseas world-changing experience begin this summer, and watch God use you literally to change the world. I look forward to seeing you this summer.

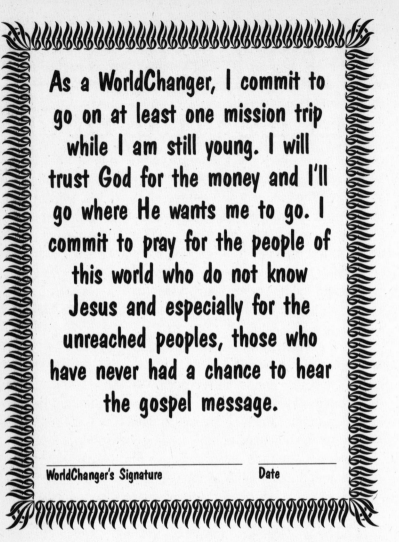

As a WorldChanger, I commit to go on at least one mission trip while I am still young. I will trust God for the money and I'll go where He wants me to go. I commit to pray for the people of this world who do not know Jesus and especially for the unreached peoples, those who have never had a chance to hear the gospel message.

_____   _____
WorldChanger's Signature   Date

WEEK 13

BLASTING INTO THE REST OF YOUR LIFE

DAY 1

CHANGE

Congratulations! You made it! I know that your life has been changed as you have applied the things suggested each day.

Let's take some time and look back to see exactly what God has done in your life. It's important to do this so you can really rejoice over what He has done. Write your answers to the following questions.

What are the two major things that God has taught you these past twelve weeks?

1. _____

2. _____

What things have changed in your life?

1. _____

2. _____

3. _____

What new habits do you have now?

1. _____

2. _____

How many Scriptures have you memorized? _____

What have you done to start changing the world?

1. _____

2. _____

3. _____

How many people have you witnessed to? _____ How many were saved? _____

Remember, it is not your responsibility to get them saved; it is your responsibility to let them know about Jesus.

"Missions is . . . 'being God's voice, hands, and feet.'"
—Jennifer

Day 2

EVALUATING
YOUR PROGRESS

Take a few minutes and read over what you wrote yesterday. Wow! Look at all the things that God has done in your life! Take some time right now and thank Him for what *He* has done through you.

In your growth in the Lord, you need to look back to really appreciate all that God is doing in your life. Yes, you must "press on" like Paul explained in Philippians 3, but you also have to see how far you have come from time to time.

Think about what has happened in your heart in the past twelve weeks. What has God been stirring up inside you? How pure is your heart these days? With all the Scriptures you have memorized and all the time you have spent in prayer, how has your passion for Jesus increased?

What about your mind? What do you spend your time thinking about? When your mind drifts off, where does it go? (I know your mom and dad would like to know this, too.) I am hoping that considering all you have learned, your mind now gets into the deep things of God.

What about your strength? How are you using it for God? How are you expressing your love for Him with your energy?

I am so proud of you, and I know that God is, too!

DAY 3

WHERE DO YOU GO FROM HERE?

Now it's time to focus on what to do with the rest of your life. You have just succeeded in a great accomplishment, and now is not the time to let down. Sometimes when you are at the top and you really succeed at something, you feel that you can back off a little. It is easy to think you can live on "yesterday's manna."

Just look at David. He had won all those wars. He had made the whole kingdom his. He had killed the bear, the lion, and Goliath. He was coasting on his victories, and instead of going out and winning more, he let the army go out on their own to fight. (Kings never did that back then; they always led the troops.) That is when he saw Bathsheba, and he blew it big time!

You can't quit fighting the fight of faith now! This is only the beginning! WorldChangers don't back off; they go on to win other victories. Look at Hebrews 10:39: "We are not like those people who turn back and get destroyed. We will keep on having faith until we are saved" (CEV).

This is not just a thirteen-week devotional; this is a lifestyle. This is not a whim; it is serious Christianity. This is not just a good idea; this is a recipe for a great life with God!

Day 4

PROGRESS REPORT

The things that you have begun to do, you should continue for the rest of your life. You should go ahead and plan on it right now.

I want you to look at the checklist at the end of this week and begin filling it in each week to show the progress you are making in each of the ten challenges of a WorldChanger.

Day 5

NO TURNING BACK

Get your heart and mind set to go for it—at least through your teen years. WorldChangers live an intense Christian lifestyle. They live all ten challenges all of their teen years. You can do it. I know. I was fired up about Jesus in my teen years, and I never turned my back on Him. Sure, I made mistakes, but I never walked away from God.

A man told me something about two weeks after I became turned on to God that totally wrecked my plans. He said that *you* can really only backslide one time in your life. I thought, *Yeah, right. I have big plans, buddy!*

He went on to explain: "When you first give your life to the Lord and then fall away accidentally, God can understand. But when you come back to the Lord, you then realize the mistake you made and you cannot do it 'accidentally' again. Now if you get away from God, you are not backsliding but intentionally turning your back on Him and walking away."

I thought, *Great! Now I don't have a choice. I have to stay on fire because I'm sure not going to intentionally turn my back on God!* So I didn't. I didn't think I had a choice. Going up and down, being on fire and falling away, was no longer an option. That man spoiled all of my plans.

Now I have just spoiled yours!

**BLASTING INTO THE
REST OF YOUR LIFE**

DAY 6

STANDING FIRM

The Bible talks about standing firm several times.

Matthew 10:22
All men will hate you because of me, but he who stands firm to the end will be saved (NIV).

Matthew 24:13
But he who stands firm to the end will be saved (NIV).

Mark 13:13
All men will hate you because of me, but he who stands firm to the end will be saved (NIV).

2 Timothy 2:12

If we endure,
We shall also reign with Him.
If we deny Him,
He also will deny us.

Being a WorldChanger is about standing firm until the end. It's about enduring, no matter what the cost.

It's not about barely making it to heaven but about blazing a trail there and taking a lot of other people with you!

It's not hoping for it; it's actually deciding to do it. It doesn't mean you are cocky just because you are determined to live right and change the world. It means you are like Jesus.

If you really do the things we've talked about in this book, you'll stand firm. I know because I do them, too.

DAY 7

**BLASTING INTO THE
REST OF YOUR LIFE**

ONLY YOU CAN DECIDE

You have joined an army of thousands of other teens in the U.S. and all over the world who are taking on the same challenge. They are tired of boring Christianity and are rising up to change the world. They are coming together as an army of young serious Christians who have decided to stand firm.

I can't make this decision for you. Your mom and dad can't decide for you. Your youth pastor can't decide for you. Even your accountability friends can't decide for you (although they can help you keep your commitment once you have made it). You have to decide on your own to stand firm.

Now is the time to get focused on how you are going to live at least through your teen years. Set your heart on your twentieth birthday. Get into your mind and heart right now the way you plan to live until then.

Make plans right now for what you will do between now and then to change the world. Think about taking over your sports team one year and overtaking your local hangouts the next year by talking about Jesus all the time. Think about the accountability friends that you want to stick with all through your teen years. Think about going on a mission trip every summer until you turn twenty. (Every summer? Yup. A lot of other teens have done it.) At least go one summer *(this year)*!

This is your chance to live free. Get into your Bible and stay there. Pick up the next Teen Mania devotional book from Thomas Nelson Publishers. (Eventually there will be four of them, to take you through a whole year.) If you haven't filled out your World-Changer 2000 certificates in the back of this book, then fill them out now and send one to us. Live a life focused on Jesus, and go crazy to get others to do the same. Make your life count while you're young.

You are a cut above this world. God's hand is on your life. You can't back down now. There is too much at stake. Get other friends turned on to becoming WorldChangers, too. You are what was prophesied about in Joel 2. You are the answer to millions of people's prayers as they have asked God to use the young people of the world.

All of history has been waiting for you to get to this point. Now all of heaven is watching to see what you will do to change the world with your life.

You must succeed; the world is counting on you. You have what it takes to make a big difference. You are a WorldChanger!

Use this to track your commitment to keep all ten challenges for Week 14 through Week 16.

1. I have been developing my relationship with Jesus and have kept my quiet times this week.
   Number of days I had my quiet time this week:

2. I have been renewing my mind and changing the way I think this week.
   Weak areas I worked on this week:

3. I have been studying my Bible and meditating on God's Word this week.
   Scriptures I meditated on this week:

4. I have been developing an accountability friendship with someone this week.
   Issues we have dealt with this week:

5. I have lived a lifestyle of worship and holy actions this week.
   Ways I worshiped or idols I cast down this week:

6. I have stayed pure this week.
   Situations in which I've stayed pure by my choices this week:

7. I have honored my parents in action and in attitude this week.
   Ways I've honored my parents this week:

8. I have attended my church and youth group this week.
   Ways I have shown commitment this week:

9. I have started a revolution in my world this week.
   Ways I have carried out the vision this week:

10. I have made preparations this week to go to the mission field.
    Preparations I have made this week:

| Date: _____ | Date: _____ | Date: _____ |
WEEK 14	**WEEK 15**	**WEEK 16**
❑	❑	❑
❑	❑	❑
❑	❑	❑
❑	❑	❑
❑	❑	❑
❑	❑	❑
❑	❑	❑
❑	❑	❑
❑	❑	❑
❑	❑	❑

Use this to track your commitment to keep all ten challenges for Week 17 through Week 19.

1. I have been developing my relationship with Jesus and have kept my quiet times this week.
   Number of days I had my quiet time this week:

2. I have been renewing my mind and changing the way I think this week.
   Weak areas I worked on this week:

3. I have been studying my Bible and meditating on God's Word this week.
   Scriptures I meditated on this week:

4. I have been developing an accountability friendship with someone this week.
   Issues we have dealt with this week:

5. I have lived a lifestyle of worship and holy actions this week.
   Ways I worshiped or idols I cast down this week:

6. I have stayed pure this week.
   Situations in which I've stayed pure by my choices this week:

7. I have honored my parents in action and in attitude this week.
   Ways I've honored my parents this week:

8. I have attended my church and youth group this week.
   Ways I have shown commitment this week:

9. I have started a revolution in my world this week.
   Ways I have carried out the vision this week:

10. I have made preparations this week to go to the mission field.
    Preparations I have made this week:

| Date: _____ | Date: _____ | Date: _____ |
WEEK 17	WEEK 18	WEEK 19
❑	❑	❑
❑	❑	❑
❑	❑	❑
❑	❑	❑
❑	❑	❑
❑	❑	❑
❑	❑	❑
❑	❑	❑
❑	❑	❑
❑	❑	❑

Use this to track your commitment to keep all ten challenges for Week 20 through Week 22.

1. I have been developing my relationship with Jesus and have kept my quiet times this week.
   Number of days I had my quiet time this week:

2. I have been renewing my mind and changing the way I think this week.
   Weak areas I worked on this week:

3. I have been studying my Bible and meditating on God's Word this week.
   Scriptures I meditated on this week:

4. I have been developing an accountability friendship with someone this week.
   Issues we have dealt with this week:

5. I have lived a lifestyle of worship and holy actions this week.
   Ways I worshiped or idols I cast down this week:

6. I have stayed pure this week.
   Situations in which I've stayed pure by my choices this week:

7. I have honored my parents in action and in attitude this week.
   Ways I've honored my parents this week:

8. I have attended my church and youth group this week.
   Ways I have shown commitment this week:

9. I have started a revolution in my world this week.
   Ways I have carried out the vision this week:

10. I have made preparations this week to go to the mission field.
    Preparations I have made this week:

Date: _____ WEEK 20	Date: _____ WEEK 21	Date: _____ WEEK 22
❑	❑	❑
❑	❑	❑
❑	❑	❑
❑	❑	❑
❑	❑	❑
❑	❑	❑
❑	❑	❑
❑	❑	❑
❑	❑	❑
❑	❑	❑

Use this to track your commitment to keep all ten challenges for Week 23 through Week 25.

1. I have been developing my relationship with Jesus and have kept my quiet times this week.
   Number of days I had my quiet time this week:

2. I have been renewing my mind and changing the way I think this week.
   Weak areas I worked on this week:

3. I have been studying my Bible and meditating on God's Word this week.
   Scriptures I meditated on this week:

4. I have been developing an accountability friendship with someone this week.
   Issues we have dealt with this week:

5. I have lived a lifestyle of worship and holy actions this week.
   Ways I worshiped or idols I cast down this week:

6. I have stayed pure this week.
   Situations in which I've stayed pure by my choices this week:

7. I have honored my parents in action and in attitude this week.
   Ways I've honored my parents this week:

8. I have attended my church and youth group this week.
   Ways I have shown commitment this week:

9. I have started a revolution in my world this week.
   Ways I have carried out the vision this week:

10. I have made preparations this week to go to the mission field.
    Preparations I have made this week:

Date: _____ **WEEK 23**	Date: _____ **WEEK 24**	Date: _____ **WEEK 25**
☐	☐	☐
☐	☐	☐
☐	☐	☐
☐	☐	☐
☐	☐	☐
☐	☐	☐
☐	☐	☐
☐	☐	☐
☐	☐	☐
☐	☐	☐

Use this to track your commitment to keep all ten challenges for Week 26 through Week 28.

1. I have been developing my relationship with Jesus and have kept my quiet times this week.
Number of days I had my quiet time this week:

2. I have been renewing my mind and changing the way I think this week.
Weak areas I worked on this week:

3. I have been studying my Bible and meditating on God's Word this week.
Scriptures I meditated on this week:

4. I have been developing an accountability friendship with someone this week.
Issues we have dealt with this week:

5. I have lived a lifestyle of worship and holy actions this week.
Ways I worshiped or idols I cast down this week:

6. I have stayed pure this week.
Situations in which I've stayed pure by my choices this week:

7. I have honored my parents in action and in attitude this week.
Ways I've honored my parents this week:

8. I have attended my church and youth group this week.
Ways I have shown commitment this week:

9. I have started a revolution in my world this week.
Ways I have carried out the vision this week:

10. I have made preparations this week to go to the mission field.
Preparations I have made this week:

| Date: _____ | Date: _____ | Date: _____ |
WEEK 26	WEEK 27	WEEK 28
❑	❑	❑
❑	❑	❑
❑	❑	❑
❑	❑	❑
❑	❑	❑
❑	❑	❑
❑	❑	❑
❑	❑	❑
❑	❑	❑
❑	❑	❑

Use this to track your commitment to keep all ten challenges for Week 29 through Week 31.

1. I have been developing my relationship with Jesus and have kept my quiet times this week.
   Number of days I had my quiet time this week:

2. I have been renewing my mind and changing the way I think this week.
   Weak areas I worked on this week:

3. I have been studying my Bible and meditating on God's Word this week.
   Scriptures I meditated on this week:

4. I have been developing an accountability friendship with someone this week.
   Issues we have dealt with this week:

5. I have lived a lifestyle of worship and holy actions this week.
   Ways I worshiped or idols I cast down this week:

6. I have stayed pure this week.
   Situations in which I've stayed pure by my choices this week:

7. I have honored my parents in action and in attitude this week.
   Ways I've honored my parents this week:

8. I have attended my church and youth group this week.
   Ways I have shown commitment this week:

9. I have started a revolution in my world this week.
   Ways I have carried out the vision this week:

10. I have made preparations this week to go to the mission field.
    Preparations I have made this week:

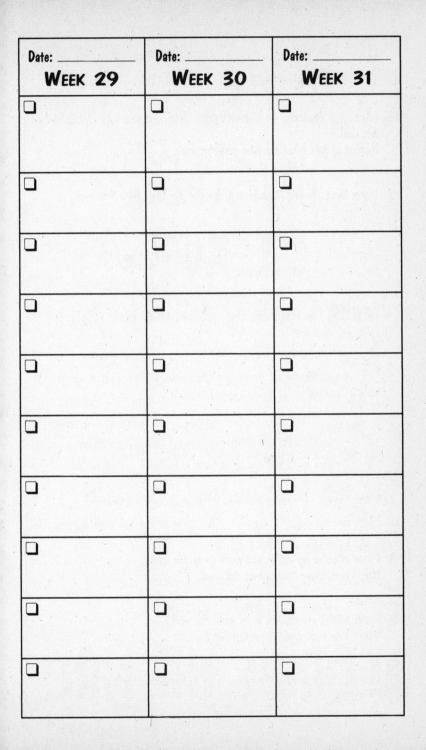

EXTREME.
IN YOUR FACE.
ETERNAL.

Finally, Something MASSIVE for You.

An explosive video wall . . . live bands . . . hilarious skits . . . and blistering pyrotechnics make an Acquire the Fire™ weekend a total blast. But more than fun. This is for REAL. Acquire the Fire conventions are about getting tight with God . . . about having a radical lifestyle of commitment to Jesus Christ . . . about living with uncompromising Christian princilple.

Acquire the Fire conventions are held in 25 cities across North America each year, reaching 100,000 teens. Call us today to find out when Acquire the Fire will be in your city. Don't miss out!

This is for you and your friends! Not just for now, but for forever.

1-800-329-FIRE

ACQUIRE THE FIRE™
CONVENTIONS

A PRESENTATION OF TEEN MANIA MINISTRIES®

WorldChangers 2000®

"Love the Lord your God with all your heart and with all your soul and with all your mind and with all your strength.' . . . 'Love your neighbor as yourself.' " (Mark 12:30-31 NIV)

WorldChangers are people who take this Scripture seriously and who live it out every day of their lives.

With All Your Heart

❏ **I commit to keep my relationship with Jesus alive by keeping my quiet times.**
❏ **I commit to systematic Bible study.**
❏ **I commit to my church and my youth group.**

With All Your Soul and with All Your Mind

❏ **I commit my mind to God.**
❏ **I commit to holy courtship instead of dating.**
❏ **I commit to honor my parents.**

With All Your Strength

❏ **I commit to an accountability friendship.**
❏ **I commit to a lifestyle of worship and holy actions.**
❏ **I commit to start a revolution.**

Love Your Neighbor as Yourself

❏ **I commit to go on a mission trip while I'm a teen.**

I commit to keep all 10 challenges throughout my teen years.

_____   _____

WorldChanger's Signature   Date

WorldChangers 2000®

"Love the Lord your God with all your heart and with all your soul and with all your mind and with all your strength.' . . . 'Love your neighbor as yourself.'" (Mark 12:30-31 NIV)

WorldChangers are people who take this Scripture seriously and who live it out every day of their lives.

With All Your Heart

- ❏ **I commit to keep my relationship with Jesus alive by keeping my quiet times.**
- ❏ **I commit to systematic Bible study.**
- ❏ **I commit to my church and my youth group.**

With All Your Soul and with All Your Mind

- ❏ **I commit my mind to God.**
- ❏ **I commit to holy courtship instead of dating.**
- ❏ **I commit to honor my parents.**

With All Your Strength

- ❏ **I commit to an accountability friendship.**
- ❏ **I commit to a lifestyle of worship and holy actions.**
- ❏ **I commit to start a revolution.**

Love Your Neighbor as Yourself

- ❏ **I commit to go on a mission trip while I'm a teen.**

I commit to keep all 10 challenges throughout my teen years.

_____   _____

WorldChanger's Signature   Date

SUMMER MISSIONS
"World Changer"
APPLICATION

Are you SERIOUS about wanting to make a commitment to take Christ to another nation next summer? Your first step is to fill out the application below and send it in. Be sure to fill out both sides

Full Name *(as written on birth certificate)*

_____

Last   First   Middle Initial

Social Security Number _____

Sex ☐ M ☐ F   Citizen of what nation? _____

Birth date ___ / ___ / ___   Age _____ Height _____ Weight _____

Permanent Address

Street _____

City _____ State/Province _____ ZIP _____

Home Phone (   ) _____

Daytime Phone (   ) _____

Current Mailing Address (if different)

Street _____

City _____ State/Province _____ ZIP _____

Phone (   ) _____ Daytime Phone (   ) _____

How long at this address and number? _____

Parent's Phone (   ) _____

List any Teen Mania missions trips you have taken:

    nation _____ date _____

    nation _____ date _____

    nation _____ date _____

Church Name _____

Church Address _____

Church Phone (   ) _____

How long have you been involved in this church? _____ years

If you are in a dating relationship with someone, is this person applying to come on this trip? ☐ Yes ☐ No

If yes, what is their name? _____

Have you ever been involved with (if so, please give date of last involvement and explanation — use additional sheet of paper if necessary)
    ☐ alcohol
    ☐ illegal drugs
    ☐ a cult or the occult

Have you ever (if so, please give date of last incident and explanation — use additional sheet of paper if necessary)
    ☐ been expelled from school?
    ☐ been placed in a juvenile detention center?
    ☐ been in jail?
    ☐ been under psychiatric care?
    ☐ had an eating disorder?
    ☐ had respiratory problems?
    ☐ had seizures/fainting spells?

Rank, in order of importance (1 being most important), any source(s) which have influenced you to come on this trip. Give names where applicable:

_____ Ron Luce	_____ Acquire the Fire Youth Convention	
_____ Regional Representative	_____ Maniac Friend	
_____ Magazine	_____ Radio/Television Program	
_____ Christian Musician	_____ TMM Intern(s)	
_____ Phone call from TMM	_____ Other	

☐ I am interested in a leadership position. Please send me an application. (Mission Advisors must be at least 18 and Team Leaders must be at least 22 years old.)

SEND WITH YOUR APPLICATION
With your application, please include the following items necessary to complete the acceptance process:
    ☐ One recent close-up nonreturnable photo of yourself — NO group shots
    ☐ $39.00 non-refundable application fee
    ☐ Parent's signature (if you're under 18)
    ☐ A one-page essay on your Christian life
        Your essay must include
            1) A description of your past and present relationship with Jesus Christ
            2) How you see your future with Him
            Write this in your own handwriting — do not type
    ☐ Pastor's recommendation

Send your application to:
TEEN MANIA MINISTRIES • P. O. Box 700721 • Tulsa, OK 74170-0721
Acceptance Department: (918) 496-1891
FAX: (918) 496-2553

GET AN
extreme
WORLDCHANGER
RUSH!

ummer is kick-back time, right? No sweat. Totally cool.

B o r i n g !

We've got something different in mind. Something totally extreme and beyond the watered-down, thumb-sucking Christianity you may have known in the past.

We want you to have a major summer rush!

You know — the kind of rush you get when you do something radical . . . when you say something that's right on target . . . when someone really listens to what you're telling them, understands it, and wants to know more!

→

We want you to join about 2,750 other kids from across North America who are going to tell the people in 15 nations about Jesus next summer. Not everyone knows who He is or why He came or what He wants to do in their lives. And that's where you come in. You go tell them!

That's where the rush comes in. From past experience, we know that a lot of these people are going to respond to the Gospel message — like about 90,000 people last year alone. Lives will be changed . . . forever. And you will be the one who helped make it happen. You will get to lead people to Jesus Christ!

What a rush!

Don't miss out. This is what "changing the world" is all about.

☎ CALL 1-800-299-TEEN

TEEN MANiA Ministries

Presented by Teen Mania®